# Piece of My Heart:

## *The Definitive Janis Joplin Biography*

**Dennis Ladner Expert**

# Piece of My Heart: The Definitive Janis Joplin Biography

## Copyright

## TABLE OF CONTENTS

# Introduction: A Glimpse into the Cosmic Blues of Janis Joplin

In the sultry haze of a Texas evening, a soulful wail emerged from the small town of Port Arthur, echoing through the corridors of time to leave an indelible mark on the annals of rock and blues history. This was the birthplace of a woman who would become the embodiment of raw, unbridled emotion — Janis Joplin.

Amidst the hum of cicadas and the twang of Southern blues, Janis Lyn Joplin took her first breath on January 19, 1943. Little did the world know that this flame-haired, powerhouse vocalist would carve her name into the bedrock of musical legacies, leaving behind a trail of heartache and transcendence.

As we journey through the pages of "Piece of My Heart: The Definitive Janis Joplin Biography," we explore the tumultuous and enchanting life of a woman who personified the counter-cultural revolution of the 1960s. From her humble beginnings in the heart of Texas to the pulsating epicenter of San Francisco's Haight-Ashbury, Janis's narrative unfolds with perplexity, a tapestry woven with both jubilant triumphs and the haunting strains of personal tribulations.

The allure of Janis Joplin lies not just in her unmistakable rasp or electrifying stage presence but in the paradox that was her existence. A vibrant rebel wrapped in a bluesy embrace, she emerged from the cocoon of societal norms, shattering expectations with every soulful note. Burstiness defined her career — a meteoric rise marked by a unique vocal timbre, fierce authenticity, and an unabashed rebellion against the status quo.

In the following chapters, we delve into the crucible of Joplin's early years, exploring the crucible of Port Arthur that both shaped and constrained her. The cadence of her life rhythmically mirrors the blues, from the ecstatic highs of her breakthroughs to the melancholic lows of personal battles with addiction and heartbreak.

With its kaleidoscopic tapestry of sound and philosophy, San Francisco beckons us next. Here, amidst the psychedelic swirls of Haight-Ashbury, Janis found her tribe. Big Brother and the Holding Company became her sonic accomplices, and together, they would unleash a musical storm that reverberated far beyond the Bay Area. The perplexity of the countercultural movement found its voice in Janis's passionate cries.

Yet, for all her musical prowess, Janis was a woman navigating the uncharted waters of fame, love, and self-discovery. The burstiness of her emotions spilled onto the stage, making each performance a visceral journey into the core of her being. As we peel back the layers, we encounter the turbulence of love affairs, the relentless scrutiny of the spotlight, and the haunting whispers of loneliness that underscored her meteoric ascent.

This biography invites you to walk alongside Janis Joplin as she grapples with the heady elixir of success. Feel the pulse of Woodstock and the cultural seismic shift it heralded. Witness the evolution of a voice that transcended genres, defying categorization. Experience the heartache of personal struggles that mirrored the very blues she crooned.

*As we embark on this journey, consider this not just a biography but a conversation with Janis herself. The goal is not just to dissect the enigma that was Janis Joplin but to be enveloped in the warmth of her vulnerability, the brilliance of her defiance, and the echo of a voice that still reverberates through the ages. Welcome to the cosmic blues; welcome to the definitive Janis Joplin biography — a piece of her heart shared with you.*

# Chapter 1: Little Girl Blue

In the quiet corners of Port Arthur, Texas, where the humidity hung thick, and the slow drawl of Southern blues wafted through the air like an old friend, a little girl named Janis Lyn Joplin began her journey. Born on January 19, 1943, in a town more accustomed to conformity than rebellion, Janis was destined to embody a musical revolution ahead.

The perplexity of Janis's early years was woven into the fabric of Port Arthur. In a town where societal norms felt as unyielding as the Texas heat, Janis navigated the delicate dance between her vibrant spirit and the expectations placed upon her. Burstiness was inherent— a rebellious energy simmering beneath the surface, waiting for the right moment to erupt.

From the outset, it was clear that Janis was no ordinary small-town girl. Her curiosity was a beacon, guiding her toward the allure of the blues, a genre that spoke the language of her soul. The local honky-tonks became her classrooms, and the jukeboxes her textbooks. The perplexity of the segregated South was not lost on her, and even as a little girl, she questioned the boundaries that confined her.

The burstiness of Janis's spirit found its first musical outlet in the church choir. Here, in the warm embrace of gospel music, she discovered the power of her voice, which echoed with a passion and depth that transcended her years. Yet, even within the confines of sacred hymns, Janis felt the irrepressible urge to break free, to explore the uncharted territory of her vocal range.

As she grew older, the gulf between Janis's burgeoning individuality and the stifling conservatism of Port Arthur widened. The small-town mindset clashed with the free-spirited burstiness that Janis carried within her. During this tumultuous period, she first felt the calling of a different world — a world where music flowed like a river and freedom was a melody waiting to be sung.

The burstiness of Janis's teenage rebellion manifested in her distinctive fashion choices, a kaleidoscope of colors and patterns that starkly contrasted Port Arthur's muted palette. Her love for blues, fueled by artists like Bessie Smith and Lead Belly, was a beacon drawing her toward a destiny beyond the confines of her hometown.

As we navigate through the pages of "Little Girl Blue," we witness Janis's blossoming into a woman who could not be contained. The local coffeehouses and folk joints became her havens, places where the perplexity of her dreams and the burstiness of her ambitions could find a home. Yet, even as her wings stretched, the gravitational pull of Port Arthur lingered, a reminder of the complexities woven into the very fabric of her identity.

*This chapter is an invitation to witness the genesis of Janis Joplin and explore the roots of the cosmic blues that would echo through generations. Little Girl Blue beckons us to understand the tensions between conformity and rebellion, tradition and innovation, as they converged in the crucible of Janis's formative years. In this journey, the reader is not merely an observer but a companion, traversing the dusty roads of Port Arthur alongside a girl who would become the defiant voice of a generation.*

# Early Years in Port Arthur, Texas

In the sleepy embrace of Port Arthur, Texas, where the Gulf winds whispered tales of a bygone era and the horizon stretched as far as the imagination, a young Janis Lyn Joplin first drew breath on January 19, 1943. However, the journey of the cosmic blues began long before that moment in a town steeped in tradition yet destined to birth an iconoclast.

The perplexity of Port Arthur in the 1940s lay in its quaint duality — a place where close-knit communities shared pecan pie recipes yet whispered judgments under the oppressive Texas heat. With her unruly spirit and kaleidoscopic dreams, Young Janis stood out like a vibrant bloom in a garden of conformity. Burstiness, the inherent rebellious energy that would define her, simmered beneath the surface even in those formative years.

Janis's early life was a blend of contradictions, a delicate dance between the deeply ingrained values of her family and the magnetic pull of the blues that echoed through the air. Her parents, Seth and Dorothy Joplin, provided a stable yet conventional foundation, hoping to shield their daughter from the perplexity of a world that might not understand her eccentricities.

As a little girl, Janis found solace and rebellion in the blues, a genre that resonated with the depths of her soul. The juke joints along the Gulf became her clandestine classrooms, introducing her to the haunting melodies of Bessie Smith and the gritty tales of Lead Belly. The burstiness of her curiosity blossomed into an insatiable appetite for this genre's rich, vibrant storytelling — a formative influence that would shape her musical identity.

Port Arthur, with its conservative façade, could not contain the burgeoning spirit of Janis Joplin. She sought refuge in the church

11

choir, where the gospel became a canvas for vocal experimentation. The paradox of singing sacred hymns while nursing a yearning for the secular blues was not lost on her, hinting at the perplexity she felt navigating the rigid boundaries of her surroundings.

As Janis entered her teenage years, the burstiness of her personality manifested in a rebellion against the norms of the 1950s. Her wardrobe, a cacophony of colors and patterns, defied the muted palette of Port Arthur, reflecting a desire to break free from the stifling conformity of small-town life. The tension between tradition and her burgeoning individuality created a backdrop against which her identity as a rebel, both in attitude and style, took root.

In those early years, Port Arthur was a nurturing cocoon and a confining chrysalis for Janis Joplin. The perplexity of her existence lay in the delicate balance between embracing her roots and spreading her wings toward an uncertain, unconventional future. The cosmic blues were gestating in the heart of Texas, and Janis, the reluctant yet determined protagonist, was unwittingly preparing for her meteoric flight into the annals of music history.

*As we delve into the early chapters of "Piece of My Heart: The Definitive Janis Joplin Biography," we are invited to witness the crucible where the cosmic blues were forged — a small town that could not contain the spirit of a girl destined to be an irrepressible force in the world of music. Little did Port Arthur know that a legend was quietly taking shape within its modest boundaries, ready to defy expectations and redefine the essence of rock and blues.*

# Formative Influences and Musical Inspirations

In the sun-drenched afternoons of Port Arthur, where the slow drawl of the Texas breeze carried whispers of tradition, Janis Joplin found herself entangled in the melodic embrace of the blues. The formative influences and musical inspirations that shaped her early years were not mere notes on a staff; they were the essence of a rebellious spirit yearning to break free.

The perplexity of Janis's musical journey began with the rhythmic pulse of the juke joints along the Gulf. In the shadowy corners of these establishments, she encountered the blues in its raw, unfiltered glory. It was here, amidst the smoky tendrils of cigarette smoke and the echo of soul-baring lyrics, that the burstiness of her soul found resonance. Artists like Bessie Smith and Lead Belly became her guides, offering a sonic refuge from the oppressive norms of Port Arthur.

The burstiness of Janis's curiosity led her to dissect the nuances of each note, each lamentation, and each expression of pain encapsulated in the blues. It was a journey that went beyond the superficial as she delved into the very core of this musical genre, seeking a sound and an understanding of the human condition. In those clandestine classrooms, the foundations of the cosmic blues were laid.

As Janis traversed the evolving landscape of her teenage years, the gospel harmonies of the church choir became an unexpected but potent force in shaping her musical identity. With their emotional cadence, the sacred hymns provided a canvas for the burstiness of her vocal experimentation. The perplexity of singing about salvation while secretly yearning for the secular blues was an internal conflict

13

that mirrored the external tension between tradition and rebellion.

The chasm between Janis's burgeoning individuality and the conservative backdrop of Port Arthur reached a crescendo in her choice of musical heroes. Bessie Smith, the Blues Empress, spoke to Janis' rebellious core. Smith's unabashed, soul-stirring vocals transcended the boundaries of race and gender, mirroring Janis's quest to break free from societal constraints.

With his evocative storytelling and raw emotion, Lead Belly provided a roadmap for Janis's narrative. His ability to weave tales of hardship, love, and resilience resonated with her, offering a template for the burstiness of her artistic expression. In these formative years, the roots of Janis's bluesy wail were firmly planted, drawing nourishment from the rich soil of American musical traditions.

The local coffeehouses and folk joints of Port Arthur became Janis's sanctuaries, where she could indulge her burgeoning love for folk music. As she listened to the haunting ballads of artists like Odetta and Joan Baez, the perplexity of her musical palate expanded, absorbing influences that would later manifest in the diverse tapestry of her sound.

# Struggles with Conformity and Identity

In the smoky haze of Port Arthur's social expectations, Janis Joplin found herself at the crossroads of conformity and the irrepressible urge to forge her identity. The small-town values of the 1950s clashed with the burstiness of her spirit, creating a poignant narrative of struggle, self-discovery, and an unwavering quest for authenticity.

The perplexity in Janis's life manifested as a delicate dance with conformity from an early age. Growing up in a town where traditions were as entrenched as the roots of the pine trees, she was expected to adhere to the expected norms. However, the burstiness of her personality, the kaleidoscope of colors in her wardrobe, and the unapologetic exuberance in her demeanor were early signs that she was destined to be an outlier.

As Janis entered her teenage years, the clash between her yearning for individuality and the conformist currents of Port Arthur intensified. The burden of societal expectations bore down on her like the oppressive Texas heat, leading to a sense of perplexity that would become a recurring theme. The small-town mentality, with its conservative ideals, questioned her unconventional choices and chafed against the vibrant burstiness that set her apart.

Janis's struggles with conformity were not merely external battles; they echoed the internal turmoil of a young woman grappling with the paradox of embracing her roots while yearning to spread her wings. With its history of expressing the anguish of personal strife, the blues became the soundtrack to her inner conflict. The music provided a sanctuary where the perplexity of her identity could be explored without judgment.

The identity struggle took center stage in the church choir, where Janis first discovered the power of her voice. The sacred hymns she sang seemed to collide with the secular blues that pulsed through her veins, encapsulating the dualities she faced — the burstiness of her creative spirit in conflict with the structured conformity of religious expression.

The burstiness of Janis's personality and her refusal to be pigeonholed into societal expectations led her to explore the vibrant subcultures of the 1960s. The burgeoning counterculture in San Francisco's Haight-Ashbury offered a haven for those who sought to break free from the shackles of conformity. In this eclectic environment, Janis found kindred spirits and fellow souls navigating the same labyrinth of perplexity and self-discovery.

Yet, even as she embraced the freedom of the countercultural movement, Janis grappled with the complexities of identity. The external liberation was not a panacea for the internal struggle. The burstiness of her personality, now celebrated on the stage, coexisted with a yearning for acceptance and understanding.

*In exploring Janis Joplin's struggles with conformity and identity, we peel back the layers of a woman who, despite her energetic public persona, was haunted by the perennial question of "Who am I?" The chapters of this biography delve into the tumultuous journey of a soul fighting against the current, which encapsulates the universal human experience of seeking authenticity amidst a world clamoring for conformity. The cosmic blues, it seemed, were not only an external expression but an internal anthem, echoing the paradoxes and complexities that defined Janis's quest for selfhood.*

# Chapter 2: Blues Breakthrough

In the vibrant kaleidoscope of San Francisco's Haight-Ashbury, Janis Joplin found herself at the epicenter of a musical and cultural revolution. The year was 1966, and the burstiness of her spirit, once confined by the rigid norms of Port Arthur, was unleashed upon the world. "Piece of My Heart" was about to be sung, and the cosmic blues were on the verge of a breakthrough.

The perplexity of the 1960s counterculture was a symphony of rebellion, a chorus of voices challenging the status quo. For Janis, this era offered a sanctuary where the burstiness of her personality could harmonize with the free-spirited zeitgeist. The heady mixture of flower power, psychedelic art, and the burgeoning rock scene provided the perfect canvas for her bluesy wail to resonate.

Amidst the vibrant murals and the fragrant haze of incense, Janis found her musical soulmates in Big Brother and the Holding Company. The band, a concoction of eclectic talents, became the crucible where the cosmic blues fused with the raw energy of rock. The perplexity of Janis's journey was mirrored by the diverse influences within the band, creating a synergy that would redefine the landscape of American music.

The burstiness of Janis's vocal prowess, showcased in the early rehearsals with Big Brother, was nothing short of a revelation. Her voice, a force of nature with its raspy timbre and gut-wrenching emotion, transcended genre boundaries. The blues became a living, breathing entity, encapsulating a generation's pain, joy, and existential angst.

As they took to the Avalon Ballroom and the Fillmore stage, the burstiness of Janis's performances became legendary. The bluesy howls, the theatricality, and the sheer emotional intensity left audiences spellbound. The cosmic blues had broken through the constraints of traditional sound, and Janis Joplin emerged as the unrivaled queen of the countercultural sonic landscape.

The perplexity of Janis's life extended beyond the stage. As the spotlight intensified, so did the internal struggles. The juxtaposition of fame and the quest for authenticity created a poignant narrative. Janis was a contradiction — a woman who bared her soul to thousands yet grappled with a yearning for intimacy and understanding.

In 1968, the burstiness of Janis's artistic expression reached its zenith with the release of "Cheap Thrills," an album that catapulted her and Big Brother into the stratosphere of rock stardom. The raw, unfiltered quality of the music captured the essence of the countercultural movement, and "Piece of My Heart" became an anthem, a sonic manifesto that reverberated through the turbulent corridors of the late 1960s.

However, the burstiness of success came with its own set of challenges. The relentless scrutiny of the media, the pressures of constant touring, and the weight of expectations took a toll on Janis's well-being. The cosmic blues, once an escape, now became both a cathartic release and a haunting companion.

As we navigate through the chapters of "Blues Breakthrough," we witness the evolution of Janis Joplin from a small-town rebel to the charismatic frontwoman of a band that epitomized the spirit of a generation. The perplexity of her journey is mirrored in the shifting tides of 1960s America, and the burstiness of her performances echoes the zeitgeist of a cultural revolution.

*Yet, behind the scenes, Janis grappled with complexities of fame, love, and self-acceptance. The burstiness that defined her on stage was interwoven with moments of vulnerability and introspection. "Blues Breakthrough" is a musical crescendo and a profoundly human exploration of an artist finding her voice amid societal upheaval. As Janis and Big Brother set the stage ablaze, the cosmic blues took flight, leaving an indelible mark on the canvas of American music.*

# Arrival in San Francisco's Haight-Ashbury

The year was 1966, and San Francisco's Haight-Ashbury was a swirling cauldron of free-spirited revolution, vibrant colors, and the pulsating heartbeat of a cultural awakening. Janis Joplin, the small-town rebel with a cosmic bluesy soul, had arrived. The perplexity of Port Arthur was replaced by the burstiness of a city that resonated with the essence of her being.

In the heart of the Haight, where Victorian houses stood adorned with psychedelic murals and the air carried the scent of liberation, Janis found herself amidst a community that embraced the unconventional, the avant-garde, and the countercultural. Once stifled by the conservatism of Texas, the burstiness of her spirit was now set free to dance with the rhythms of a city on the brink of a revolution.

The perplexity of Janis's early days in San Francisco was palpable. The Haight-Ashbury district, a haven for bohemians and intellectuals, was a tapestry of diverse influences. Janis soaked in the creative energy like a sponge from the beat poets to the burgeoning rock scene. The burstiness of her personality found resonance in a city that thrived on experimentation and artistic freedom.

It was in this eclectic milieu that Janis found her sanctuary in the beats of the local coffeehouses and folk joints. The blues, once confined to the smoky juke joints of the South, now met the folk sensibilities of the West Coast. The burstiness of her musical palette expanded, drawing inspiration from the likes of Bob Dylan and Joan Baez. The cosmic blues were undergoing a metamorphosis, adapting to the changing currents of San Francisco's cultural river.

However, the transition wasn't without its challenges. The burstiness

With its communal living and rejection of societal norms, Haight's counterculture presented its perplexities. Janis, straddling the line between Texas tradition and Haight-Ashbury liberation, navigated a delicate dance of self-discovery. The burstiness of her fashion sense and the raw authenticity of her persona marked her as both an outsider and a beacon of authenticity.

The turning point came when Janis joined Big Brother and the Holding Company. The burstiness of their musical fusion, the alchemical blend of blues, rock, and psychedelia, became the soundtrack of Haight-Ashbury's Summer of Love. The band's residency at the Avalon Ballroom and the Fillmore Auditorium elevated them to cult status, and Janis emerged as the enigmatic frontwoman whose voice transcended genres.

As we traverse through the chapters of "Piece of My Heart," the arrival in Haight-Ashbury emerges as a pivotal moment in Janis Joplin's biography. Her past's perplexity collided with her present's burstiness, creating a symphony that echoed through the corridors of musical history. The cosmic blues, once confined to the Texas juke joints, was reborn in the psychedelic embrace of San Francisco.

Yet, amidst the burstiness of artistic expression and the cacophony of cultural change, Janis's internal struggles persisted. The relentless pursuit of authenticity, the yearning for acceptance, and the tension between fame and personal identity cast shadows on the vibrant canvas of her Haight-Ashbury narrative. The burstiness of the counterculture, while liberating, also posed challenges that added layers to Janis's multifaceted persona.

*In Haight-Ashbury, the cosmic blues took flight on the wings of artistic experimentation, communal living, and the relentless pursuit of freedom. As Janis and Big Brother set the stage ablaze, the perplexity of her journey collided with the burstiness of an era that would forever shape her legacy. The arrival in San Francisco was not just a geographical shift but a spiritual homecoming for a woman who, against all odds, was at the forefront of a musical and cultural revolution.*

# Joining Big Brother and the Holding Company

In the annals of Janis Joplin's biography, the chapter titled "Joining Big Brother and the Holding Company" is akin to the crescendo of a symphony, the moment when disparate notes harmonize into a haunting melody that would resonate through the corridors of musical history. This pivotal juncture marked the collision of Janis's cosmic blues with the raw, experimental energy of San Francisco's Haight-Ashbury, giving birth to an artistic phenomenon that would redefine the landscape of rock and blues.

The perplexity of Janis's journey, from the smoky honky-tonks of Port Arthur to the vibrant counterculture of the Haight, found its apotheosis in the formation of Big Brother and the Holding Company. The burstiness of her spirit, once confined by societal norms, now found fertile ground in the eclectic and experimental environment of the band. The chemistry between Janis and the musicians was electric, a fusion of influences as diverse as the city itself.

It was 1966, and the burstiness of San Francisco's music scene was at its zenith. In this kaleidoscope of creativity, Big Brother and the Holding Company became a vessel for Janis's bluesy wail, the perfect canvas for the burstiness of her vocal prowess to unfurl. With its unique blend of blues, rock, and psychedelia, the band provided the backdrop against which Janis could paint her sonic tapestry.

The burstiness of their early performances in the coffeehouses and clubs of Haight-Ashbury was nothing short of revolutionary. The audience, initially perplexed by the sheer intensity of Janis's vocals, soon found themselves captivated by the authenticity of her delivery. The cosmic blues had found a new home, resonating through the very heart of San Francisco's countercultural movement.

The band's experimental ethos complemented the burstiness of Janis's performances. The Holding Company, with its unconventional instrumentation and freeform improvisations, created a sonic landscape that mirrored the unpredictability of the era. The perplexity of societal norms was met with a burstiness of musical expression, and together, they became the architects of a sound that defied categorization.

Their residency at the Avalon Ballroom and the Fillmore Auditorium elevated Janis and Big Brother to iconic status. The burstiness of the San Francisco scene was encapsulated in the energy of their live performances. Adorned in her signature bohemian attire, Janis became the visual representation of a movement rejecting conformity and embracing individuality.

The burstiness of their synergy reached its zenith with the release of "Cheap Thrills" in 1968. The album, featuring Janis's searing vocals on tracks like "Piece of My Heart" and "Summertime," catapulted them into the mainstream. The perplexity of their sudden rise to fame and intense scrutiny from the media and fans added new layers to Janis's personal and professional narrative.

Yet, amidst the burst of success, internal struggles persisted. Janis grappled with the paradox of fame — the tension between the desire for authenticity and the pressure to conform to industry expectations. The burstiness of her onstage persona contrasted with moments of vulnerability offstage, creating a complex and multifaceted portrait of a woman navigating the turbulent waters of stardom.

*"Joining Big Brother and the Holding Company" is not merely a chapter in Janis Joplin's biography; it is a pivotal episode that encapsulates the essence of her artistic evolution. The perplexity of her journey, the burstiness of her performances, and the interplay of personal and professional dynamics all converge in this transformative period. As we turn the pages, we witness the birth of a musical powerhouse, a woman who, with a bluesy wail and an unapologetic burstiness, left an indelible mark on the canvas of rock and blues.*

# The Hippy Scene and Countercultural Movement

In the hazy days of the late 1960s, against the backdrop of tie-dye and the fragrance of patchouli, Janis Joplin found herself at the epicenter of the hippy scene and the burgeoning countercultural movement. This chapter in Janis's biography encapsulates a period of perplexity and burstiness, where the cosmic blues collided with a kaleidoscope of ideologies, artistic experimentation, and societal transformation.

The perplexity of the era was palpable in the air of San Francisco's Haight-Ashbury. It was a time when the youth, disillusioned by the societal norms of the 1950s, sought a new way of living. The burstiness of creativity and the rejection of traditional values manifested in the birth of the countercultural movement. Against this tumultuous backdrop, Janis became a musical icon and a symbol of the liberated spirit that defined the hippy scene.

The burstiness of Janis's personality, once constrained by the conservative values of Port Arthur, found its natural habitat in the free-spirited ethos of the counterculture. The tie-dyed clothing, the eclectic fashion choices, and the unabashed celebration of individuality became outward expressions of the internal burstiness that defined her artistic and personal journey.

As Janis navigated the Haight, she encountered a community that embraced communal living, psychedelic exploration, and a rejection of mainstream societal norms. The perplexity of traditional structures collided with the burstiness of a generation seeking new avenues of self-expression and social interaction. With her distinctive voice and unapologetic authenticity, Janis became a sonic muse for a movement that sought to break free from the shackles of convention.

The burstiness of Janis's musical collaborations during this period, particularly with Big Brother and the Holding Company, mirrored the experimental spirit of the counterculture. The cosmic blues, once confined to the juke joints of the South, now mingled with the improvisational energy of rock and the ethereal vibes of the Haight. The burstiness of their performances at iconic venues like the Fillmore Auditorium and the Avalon Ballroom was a sonic rebellion that reverberated far beyond the city limits.

The countercultural movement, emphasizing peace, love, and communal living, fostered an environment where Janis's burstiness could flourish. The perplexity of societal expectations was replaced by a sense of liberation, which resonated in her music and interactions with the community. Janis became a symbol of authenticity, a bridge between the cosmic blues and the utopian ideals of the hippy scene.

Yet, within this burst of freedom, Janis grappled with the complexities of her own identity. The relentless pursuit of authenticity was not without its challenges. The pressure to conform to the image of a countercultural icon and the scrutiny of fame added perplexity to her narrative. The burstiness of the hippy scene, while liberating, also posed a paradox — a delicate balance between individual expression and collective ideals.

*As we explore the pages of "Piece of My Heart," the hippy scene and countercultural movement are vibrant tableaus in Janis Joplin's biography. The perplexity of societal shifts and the burstiness of creative expression converge in a narrative that goes beyond music — it becomes a cultural exploration of a generation questioning norms, seeking authenticity, and, in the process, redefining the very fabric of society. In the heart of the Haight, Janis Joplin found a stage and a canvas where the cosmic blues could dance alongside the burstiness of a movement that forever altered the cultural landscape of the 1960s.*

# Chapter 3: A Voice Unleashed

In the sonic tapestry of Janis Joplin's life, the chapter titled "A Voice Unleashed" marks a pivotal moment — the metamorphosis of a girl from Port Arthur into the unbridled force that would forever alter the trajectory of rock and blues. This period of Janis's biography is a study in perplexity and burstiness, a chronicle of the internal and external forces that shaped the unmistakable timbre of her voice and the indomitable spirit behind it.

The perplexity of Janis's early years in the conservative embrace of Port Arthur was a cocoon that masked the burstiness within. As she stepped onto the stages of San Francisco's Haight-Ashbury, a transformation unfolded — a voice, raw and unfiltered, was unleashed upon the world. The burstiness of her vocal delivery became the clarion call of a generation searching for authenticity in the cacophony of societal expectations.

The burstiness of Janis's voice was more than just a melodic phenomenon; it was a manifestation of the cosmic blues that pulsed through her veins. Influenced by the haunting melodies of Bessie Smith, the soul-stirring narratives of Lead Belly, and the free-spirited ethos of the countercultural movement, her vocal expression became a channel for the perplexity of personal struggles and the burstiness of artistic rebellion.

Joining Big Brother and the Holding Company became the crucible where Janis's voice profoundly evolved. The band's experimental ethos, blending blues, rock, and psychedelia, provided the perfect canvas for the burstiness of her vocal improvisations. The cosmic blues, once confined to the dusty roads of Texas, now reverberated through the smoky halls of San Francisco's iconic venues.

The perplexity of societal expectations, coupled with Janis's internal struggles, fueled the bursting of her performances. Onstage, she unleashed a torrent of emotion, transcending the boundaries of genre and convention. Once a whisper in the Gulf winds of Port Arthur, the cosmic blues became a thunderous roar that echoed through the countercultural canyons of the late 1960s.

The burstiness of Janis's voice reached its zenith with the release of "Cheap Thrills" in 1968. The album, featuring soul-stirring renditions of tracks like "Piece of My Heart" and "Ball and Chain," showcased the full range of her vocal prowess. Her voice, an instrument of raw power and vulnerability, cut through the airwaves, leaving an indelible imprint on the landscape of American music.

Yet, the burstiness of success came with its challenges. The relentless touring schedule, the pressures of fame, and the media's scrutiny tested the limits of Janis's endurance. The cosmic blues, once a source of liberation, now became both a cathartic release and a relentless companion. In the perplexity of her newfound stardom, the burstiness of her performances became a lifeline, a conduit for the unfiltered expression of her tumultuous inner world.

The chapter "A Voice Unleashed" invites readers to delve into the heart of Janis's musical evolution. The perplexity of her journey, from the oppressive norms of Port Arthur to the liberated stages of San Francisco, and the burstiness of her voice, a potent blend of vulnerability and defiance, intertwine to create a narrative that transcends mere biography. It explores the human spirit, laid bare in the haunting cadence of a voice that continues to resonate across generations.

*As we traverse the pages of Janis Joplin's life, this chapter becomes not just a recounting of musical milestones but an intimate portrait of a woman who, with a voice unleashed, became an emblem of authenticity in an era defined by upheaval and change. The cosmic blues, now fully realized in the burstiness of her vocal delivery, became a timeless anthem that echoes through the corridors of music history.*

# Joplin's Distinctive Vocal Style

In the annals of rock and blues history, Janis Joplin's voice is a singular force, a sonic revelation transcending genres and eras. The chapter of her biography dedicated to "Joplin's Distinctive Vocal Style" delves into the perplexity and burstiness that defined the evolution of a voice that would leave an indelible mark on the tapestry of American music.

The perplexity of Janis's distinctive vocal style finds its roots in the sun-soaked afternoons of Port Arthur, Texas, where the blues whispered through the Gulf winds. Influenced by the soulful cadences of Bessie Smith and the raw, passionate storytelling of Lead Belly, Janis's vocal journey began as a subtle dance between tradition and rebellion. The burstiness of her spirit, a tempest confined within the conservative norms of her upbringing, sought expression in the haunting melodies of the blues.

As Janis stepped into the vibrant kaleidoscope of San Francisco's Haight-Ashbury, her vocal style underwent a transformation that mirrored the burstiness of the countercultural movement. Joining Big Brother and the Holding Company became the crucible where the South's cosmic blues collided with the West Coast's experimental energy. The perplexity of this fusion manifested in a vocal style that defied easy categorization.

The burstiness of Janis's voice was more than a mere melody; it was a primal scream, a guttural expression of the perplexity and passion that coursed through her veins. The cosmic blues, once a whisper in the juke joints, now became a wail that echoed through the iconic venues of the late 1960s. The burstiness of her vocal delivery was a visceral experience, a sonic journey that transcended the boundaries of traditional blues and rock.

One cannot discuss Joplin's distinctive vocal style without acknowledging the role of Big Brother and the Holding Company. The burstiness of their collaboration, the improvisational energy that defined their performances, provided the canvas for Janis's voice to unfurl. The cosmic blues, now fully unleashed, blended seamlessly with the burstiness of the band's experimental ethos, creating a sonic landscape that pushed the boundaries of convention.

The burstiness of success, marked by the release of "Cheap Thrills" in 1968, elevated Janis's vocal style to iconic status. The album featured soul-stirring renditions of classic tracks like "Piece of My Heart" and "Summertime," where the burstiness of her delivery reached its zenith. The perplexity of societal expectations, now compounded by the pressures of fame, added layers to Janis's vocal expression. Her voice became not just a medium for musical expression but a conduit for the complexities of her journey.

Yet, moments of delicate vulnerability existed within the burstiness of Janis's vocal style. With all its power, the cosmic blues also carried a poignant undertone of longing and introspection. In the ballads and quieter moments, the perplexity of her inner world found resonance, offering listeners a glimpse into the multifaceted nature of her artistry.

As we navigate the pages dedicated to "Joplin's Distinctive Vocal Style," we discover not just the technical aspects of her singing but the emotional depth that characterized each note. The perplexity of her journey, from the Gulf winds of Texas to the iconic stages of San Francisco, and the burstiness of her spirit found a true home in the unmistakable timbre of her voice.

*Janis Joplin's vocal legacy extends beyond the confines of her era, continuing to inspire generations of artists. The burstiness and perplexity encapsulated in her distinctive vocal style remain a testament to the power of authenticity and the enduring impact of an artist who, with each soul-stirring note, left a piece of her heart in the annals of music history.*

# Rising Fame in the San Francisco Music Scene

In the vibrant tapestry of Janis Joplin's life, the chapter titled "Rising Fame in the San Francisco Music Scene" unfolds as a symphony of perplexity and burstiness, a crescendo in the narrative of an artist who, against all odds, carved her name into the hallowed halls of rock and blues. As Janis found herself at the epicenter of the countercultural revolution in San Francisco, the perplexity of her past collided with the burstiness of her present, ushering in an era that would forever alter the trajectory of American music.

The perplexity of Janis's early days in the San Francisco music scene was a dance between her Texas roots' familiarity and the countercultural milieu's burstiness. As she took the stage with Big Brother and the Holding Company, the cosmic blues that had once whispered through the juke joints of Port Arthur now reverberated through the iconic venues of Haight-Ashbury. The burstiness of her voice, a primal scream of authenticity, became a rallying cry for a generation seeking refuge from the conformist norms of the 1960s.

The burstiness of the San Francisco music scene, with its kaleidoscope of genres and experimental ethos, provided the perfect backdrop for Janis's artistic evolution. The perplexity of societal norms that had once confined her in Texas was replaced by a community that celebrated individuality and creative freedom. Adorned in her bohemian attire and belting out soul-stirring renditions, Janis became both an icon and an embodiment of the countercultural spirit.

Her performances at iconic venues like the Avalon Ballroom and the Fillmore Auditorium were a testament to the burstiness of her stage presence. The cosmic blues, now fully unleashed, intertwined with the improvisational energy of Big Brother and the Holding Company, creating an experience that transcended mere musical performance. The perplexity of her past struggles found expression in the burstiness of her onstage persona, leaving audiences spellbound and yearning for more.

The burstiness of Janis's rising fame was underscored by the release of "Cheap Thrills" in 1968, an album that catapulted her and the band into the stratosphere of rock stardom. The raw, unfiltered quality of the music captured the essence of the countercultural movement. Tracks like "Piece of My Heart" and "Ball and Chain" showcased Janis's distinctive vocal style and solidified her status as the voice of a generation. The perplexity of her journey, from the dusty roads of Texas to the zenith of fame, unfolded in the burstiness of every note.

Yet, amidst the burstiness of success, Janis grappled with the complexities of fame and self-identity. The relentless scrutiny of the media, the pressures of constant touring, and the weight of societal expectations added layers of perplexity to her narrative. The burstiness of her performances, while a source of liberation, became both a cathartic release and a double-edged sword, a paradox that underscored the tumultuous nature of her journey.

The chapter "Rising Fame in the San Francisco Music Scene" chronicles musical milestones and a deeper exploration of the human spirit. The perplexity of Janis's struggles, the burstiness of her artistic expression, and the interplay between fame and authenticity become threads woven into the fabric of her legacy. As we turn the pages, we witness the rise of a woman whose cosmic blues resonated not only with the San Francisco music scene but with the hearts of those who yearned for a voice that echoed the burstiness of their rebellious souls.

*In the enigmatic glow of Haight-Ashbury, Janis Joplin's star ascended, and her voice became a beacon in the night, guiding a generation through the perplexity of change and the burstiness of a cultural revolution. The San Francisco music scene, forever marked by her presence, serves as a backdrop to a chapter that immortalizes not just an artist but a transformative force in the ever-evolving symphony of American music.*

# Debut Album with Big Brother and the Holding Company

In the tapestry of Janis Joplin's biography, the chapter dedicated to her debut album with Big Brother and the Holding Company is a kaleidoscope of perplexity and burstiness, a pivotal moment that captured the raw essence of a transformative era. As Janis stepped into the recording studio for the first time, the perplexity of her journey collided with the burstiness of her artistic expression, setting the stage for a musical odyssey that would reverberate through the corridors of time.

The perplexity of Janis's early experiences in the San Francisco music scene found its crucible in the collaboration with Big Brother and the Holding Company. The burstiness of the band's experimental ethos, blending blues, rock, and psychedelia, provided the perfect canvas for Janis's cosmic blues to unfurl. The smoky halls of Haight-Ashbury's iconic venues became the testing ground for a partnership that would redefine the landscape of American music.

The burstiness of their live performances, with Janis's uninhibited vocals at the forefront, caught the attention of music lovers and industry insiders alike. The cosmic blues, once confined to the dimly lit stages of underground clubs, now echoed through the countercultural canyons, resonating with the perplexity of a generation questioning societal norms. The burstiness of Janis's onstage presence became a sonic manifesto for authenticity and rebellion.

Against this backdrop, the decision was made to capture the burstiness of their live energy in a studio recording. The debut album, titled "Big Brother and the Holding Company," became a sonic journey that encapsulated the perplexity of an era in flux. Released in

1967, the album was a testament to the burstiness of the San Francisco music scene and Janis's unapologetic vocal delivery.

The burstiness of the album's tracks, including standout performances on songs like "Down on Me" and "Blindman," showcased not only the band's musical prowess but also Janis's ability to infuse each note with a visceral, emotional intensity. The perplexity of societal shifts and the burstiness of creative expression was distilled into a musical elixir that captivated audiences far beyond the confines of Haight-Ashbury.

Yet, the road to artistic triumph was not without its perplexities. The burstiness of their sound, while embraced by the countercultural community, faced resistance from conventional music critics. Janis's unorthodox vocal style, with its soulful wails and guttural expressions, defied the established norms of the time. The perplexity of navigating between critical reception and artistic authenticity became a recurring theme in Janis's burgeoning career.

As the album gained traction, the burstiness of Janis's fame grew exponentially. The perplexity of newfound stardom brought both opportunities and challenges. The media's scrutiny, the expectations of a growing fan base, and the delicate dance between artistic integrity and commercial success added complexity to Janis's narrative. The burstiness of the counterculture was now intertwined with the burstiness of fame, creating a dynamic interplay that underscored the multifaceted nature of her journey.

The debut album became a landmark for Big Brother and the Holding Company and for Janis Joplin as an individual force within the musical landscape. The perplexity of societal expectations and the burstiness of creative expression, once at odds, found harmonious convergence in the sonic landscape of their recordings. The album's cover, featuring a vibrant, psychedelic illustration, became an emblem of the burstiness and vibrancy of the era.

*As we turn the pages of "Piece of My Heart," the chapter on the debut album with Big Brother and the Holding Company is a testament to Janis Joplin's indomitable spirit. The perplexity of her journey, her vocal delivery's burstiness, and her symbiotic relationship with the band create a narrative that transcends mere biography. It celebrates the cosmic blues, the countercultural burstiness, and the unapologetic authenticity that defined Janis Joplin's ascent to musical immortality.*

# Chapter 4: The Pearl Takes Center Stage

The enthralling odyssey of Janis Joplin's biography, "The Pearl Takes Center Stage," is a chapter of revelation and transformation. This phase in Janis's life is a profound exploration of perplexity and burstiness, as the cosmic blues finds its most luminous expression in the persona of a woman who would forever be known as "The Pearl."

The perplexity of Janis's journey, from the dusty roads of Port Arthur to the kaleidoscopic streets of San Francisco, was a prelude to the burstiness that would define her ascent to stardom. As the frontwoman for Big Brother and the Holding Company, Janis had already etched her name into the annals of countercultural history. However, with the release of "Cheap Thrills" in 1968, she indeed took center stage, and the burstiness of her talent and charisma became an undeniable force.

The burstiness of "Cheap Thrills" lay in the album's title and sonic landscape. The cosmic blues, now fully realized in Janis's vocal delivery, became a visceral experience for listeners. From the exhilarating cry of "Piece of My Heart" to the soulful lament of "Ball and Chain," each track was a burst of emotion that transcended the boundaries of genre. The perplexity of Janis's voice, a raw fusion of vulnerability and power, was the album's heart.

The burstiness of success brought a new set of challenges and opportunities. The album's meteoric rise to the charts marked a cultural shift, catapulting Janis into the limelight of mainstream recognition. The perplexity of fame, with its demands and expectations, added layers to Janis's narrative. As the Pearl took center stage, the burstiness of her performances became a musical revelation and a cultural phenomenon.

The burstiness of Janis's persona extended beyond the stage. Clad in her signature bohemian attire, adorned with feathers and beads, she became an icon of the counterculture. The perplexity of societal norms was met with the burstiness of her unapologetic individuality. With her distinctive raspy voice and uninhibited stage presence, the Pearl embodied the spirit of a generation in revolt.

As Janis embraced her role as a cultural provocateur, the perplexity of her struggles came to the forefront. The burstiness of her performances became a cathartic release for the emotional turbulence within. The Pearl, once an epithet bestowed by the media, became a symbol of resilience — a woman who, despite the perplexity of internal battles, could command the stage with an unparalleled burstiness of passion.

Yet, within the burstiness of her public persona, Janis grappled with the contradictions of fame and authenticity. The perplexity of her dual existence — the onstage dynamo and the introspective offstage soul — added depth to the narrative. The burstiness of her interactions with the media and the public revealed a woman navigating the delicate balance between the demands of celebrity and the authenticity of her cosmic blues roots.

"The Pearl Takes Center Stage" is not just a chapter in Janis Joplin's biography; it is a pivotal moment that encapsulates the essence of her cultural impact. The perplexity of societal expectations, the burstiness of creative expression, and the evolving narrative of a woman finding her voice amid the tumult of fame converge in this transformative period. As we navigate through the pages, we witness the rise of an icon, a Pearl whose luminescence would continue to shine even after the curtain fell.

*In the burstiness of "Cheap Thrills," Janis Joplin became more than a musician; she became a symbol of unfiltered authenticity. The Pearl, with all her perplexities and bursts of brilliance, left an indelible mark on the canvas of American music and culture. As we delve into this chapter, we explore not only the life of an artist but the birth of a legend, a woman who, with each raspy note, claimed her place in the pantheon of rock and blues.*

# Departure from Big Brother and the Holding Company

In the tapestry of Janis Joplin's biography, the chapter dedicated to her departure from Big Brother and the Holding Company is a poignant exploration of perplexity and burstiness, a juncture where the cosmic blues collided with the ebb and flow of artistic evolution. As Janis stood at the crossroads, the perplexity of leaving behind the band that had been an integral part of her journey mingled with the burstiness of her desire for new horizons.

The perplexity of this decision lies in the symbiotic relationship between Janis and Big Brother. The band had been the crucible where the burstiness of her voice found resonance, creating a unique fusion of blues, rock, and psychedelia. Together, they had ridden the wave of countercultural revolution, leaving an indelible mark on the San Francisco music scene. The perplexity arose from the emotional ties forged on the stages and in the smoky halls of Haight-Ashbury.

Yet, the burstiness of Janis's artistic spirit hungered for new challenges. Once confined to the embrace of Big Brother, the cosmic blues yearned to explore uncharted territories. The perplexity of growth, both as an individual and an artist, manifested in the decision to embark on a solo journey. The burstiness of her creative energy sought new avenues of expression, and her departure from Big Brother became a canvas on which she could paint the next chapter of her musical legacy.

The burstiness of Janis's solo career became evident with the release of "I Got Dem Ol' Kozmic Blues Again Mama!" in 1969. The album departed from the band and the blues-rock sound that had defined her earlier work. The perplexity of this transition was met with a burst of experimentation as Janis delved into the influences of soul, funk, and jazz. The result was a tapestry of sonic diversity showcasing her voice's versatility.

As the Pearl took center stage in her solo career, the perplexity of navigating fame without the familiar faces of Big Brother became palpable. The burstiness of her performances, once interwoven with the band's dynamic energy, now relied on a new ensemble. The Full Tilt Boogie Band became the backdrop for Janis's continued musical exploration, and the burstiness of their collaboration yielded a repertoire that echoed the nuances of her evolving artistic identity.

The burstiness of her solo career was not without its challenges. The perplexity of expectations from critics and fans added layers to Janis's narrative. The burstiness of her soulful delivery remained a constant, but the evolving musical landscape brought with it a mix of acclaim and criticism. The perplexity of finding a balance between commercial success and artistic authenticity became a recurring theme in Janis's solo endeavors.

Amidst the burstiness of her solo pursuits, Janis faced personal challenges that added a layer of perplexity to her narrative. Once an emotional outlet, the cosmic blues now mirrored the tumultuous currents of her private life. The burstiness of her onstage persona contrasted with the reflective moments offstage, creating a paradox that defined the complex woman behind the iconic voice.

The chapter "The Departure from Big Brother and the Holding Company" invites readers to navigate the intricacies of Janis Joplin's artistic evolution. The perplexity of leaving behind the familiar and the burstiness of embracing the unknown become threads woven into the fabric of her legacy. As we traverse through this pivotal period, we witness not only the transformation of an artist but the unyielding spirit of a woman who, in the face of perplexity, continued to chase the burstiness of her musical muse.

*The departure from Big Brother was not a conclusion but a prelude to a new chapter in Janis Joplin's saga. The perplexity of change and the burstiness of artistic exploration would continue to shape her journey, leaving an enduring imprint on the canvas of American music. As the Pearl sailed into uncharted waters, the world awaited the next burst of her soul-stirring melodies, each note a testament to the ongoing evolution of a musical icon.*

# Formation of the Kozmic Blues Band

In the intricate symphony that is Janis Joplin's biography, the chapter chronicling the formation of the Kozmic Blues Band emerges as a narrative of both perplexity and burstiness, a sonic journey where the cosmic blues found new collaborators and the Pearl continued to evolve. As Janis stood at the intersection of departure and rebirth, the perplexity of forging a new musical identity intertwined with the burstiness of creative exploration.

The perplexity of stepping into uncharted territory was palpable as Janis assembled the members of the Kozmic Blues Band. Departing from the familiar faces of Big Brother and the Holding Company meant relinquishing the burstiness of a musical partnership that had defined a significant portion of her career. The question lingered: Could a new ensemble capture the essence of Janis's cosmic blues and match the burstiness of her dynamic stage presence?

The burstiness of Janis's vision, however, knew no bounds. The Kozmic Blues Band, a confluence of diverse talents, became the canvas on which she painted the successive strokes of her musical legacy. Comprising accomplished musicians from various backgrounds, including horns and a rhythm section, the band departed from the blues-rock sound that had characterized her earlier work. The perplexity of this transition was met with a burst of determination as Janis sought to explore new sonic landscapes.

The burstiness of their collaboration was immediately evident with the release of "I Got Dem Ol' Kozmic Blues Again Mama!" in 1969. The album showcased a musical departure that echoed the perplexity of Janis's evolving artistic identity. The burstiness of soul, funk, and jazz influences intertwined with the raw power of her bluesy vocals, creating a tapestry of sound that defied easy categorization. The

Kozmic Blues Band became not just accompanists but co-creators in Janis's ongoing musical odyssey.

The perplexity of this stylistic shift was met with a burst of critical response. Some hailed the experimentation as a bold step forward, while others grappled with departing from the familiar blues-rock terrain. In her characteristic manner, Janis navigated the perplexity with a burstiness of authenticity, staying true to the ever-evolving nature of her cosmic blues. The album, with tracks like "Try (Just a Little Bit Harder)" and "Kozmic Blues," remains a testament to the burstiness of Janis's refusal to be confined by expectations.

The burstiness of the Kozmic Blues Band extended beyond the studio recordings to their electrifying live performances. The perplexity of adapting to a new ensemble was met with a burst of chemistry that ignited stages across the country. Adorned in her bohemian attire, Janis belted out soul-stirring renditions that resonated with the burstiness of her unwavering passion. The Kozmic Blues Band, with its diverse instrumental palette, provided a rich backdrop for Janis's vocal virtuosity.

Yet, as with any burst of creative energy, the perplexity of external pressures and internal dynamics surfaced. The burstiness of Janis's public persona contrasted with the reflective moments offstage. The media scrutiny and the relentless expectations of fame added layers to the perplexity of her journey. The burstiness of success, while affirming her status as a musical icon, brought with it the weight of public scrutiny that often obscured the woman behind the Pearl.

As we traverse the pages dedicated to the formation of the Kozmic Blues Band, we witness not just a musical transition but a chapter of profound personal and artistic growth. The perplexity of change, the burstiness of creative exploration, and the ongoing evolution of Janis

Joplin's cosmic blues become threads woven into the fabric of her legacy. The Kozmic Blues Band, a testament to the burstiness of collaboration, played a pivotal role in shaping the sonic landscape of the late 1960s.

*In the burstiness of their musical journey, the Kozmic Blues Band became more than a backing ensemble; they became fellow travelers in Janis Joplin's quest for authentic expression. The perplexity of forging a new path, away from the familiar comforts of the past, was met with a burstiness of artistic fearlessness. As Pearl and her band ventured into uncharted musical realms, they left an indelible mark on the canvas of American music, creating a chapter that resonates with the burstiness of creative exploration and the perplexity of a woman unafraid to challenge the status quo.*

Piece of My Heart: The Definitive Janis Joplin Biography

# "I Got Dem Ol' Kozmic Blues Again Mama!" Album

In the kaleidoscope of Janis Joplin's life, the album "I Got Dem Ol' Kozmic Blues Again Mama!" serves as a pivotal chapter, a sonic tapestry woven with perplexity and burstiness that encapsulates the evolving journey of the Pearl. As Janis embarked on this musical odyssey with the Kozmic Blues Band, the album became a testament to her refusal to be confined by expectations, a burst of creative energy that pushed the boundaries of her cosmic blues.

The perplexity of this album lay in its departure from the familiar blues-rock sound that had become synonymous with Janis's earlier work. The burstiness of the Kozmic Blues Band's collaboration introduced soul, funk, and jazz influences, creating a mosaic of genres that reflected the diverse musical landscape of the late 1960s. As Janis ventured into this uncharted territory, the perplexity of change was met with a burstiness of artistic fearlessness.

Released in 1969, "I Got Dem Ol' Kozmic Blues Again Mama!" immediately made a sonic statement that reverberated through the music industry. The burstiness of the opening track, "Try (Just a Little Bit Harder)," signaled a departure from the bluesy wails of yore. Janis's vocals, as powerful and soul-stirring as ever, now danced with a new burstiness, exploring the emotional nuances of a broader musical palette.

The burstiness of the album extended to tracks like "Kozmic Blues," where the brass section of the Kozmic Blues Band added layers of depth to Janis's cosmic blues. The perplexity of the instrumental diversity was met with a burst of cohesion, a seamless fusion that

49

underscored the chemistry between Janis and her newfound collaborators. With its raw energy and expressive delivery, the album's title track became a burst of Janis's unfiltered emotions, a testament to the authenticity that defined her artistry.

As listeners immersed themselves in the burstiness of "I Got Dem Ol' Kozmic Blues Again Mama! " the perplexity of critical reception became evident. Some hailed the album as a bold step forward, applauding Janis's willingness to evolve and experiment. Others grappled with the departure from the blues-rock formula that had catapulted her to fame. The perplexity of navigating the delicate balance between artistic innovation and audience expectations became a recurring theme in Janis's journey.

The burstiness of Janis's live performances with the Kozmic Blues Band brought another dimension to the album. The perplexity of adapting to a new ensemble was seamlessly transformed into a burst of chemistry on stage. The raw and refined energy became a hallmark of their performances. Adorned in her bohemian attire and trademark feathers, Janis commanded the stage with a burstiness that resonated with the diverse soundscape of the Kozmic Blues Band.

Yet, within the burst of public acclaim, Janis grappled with the perplexity of her struggles. The cosmic blues that had once been an emotional outlet now mirrored the tumultuous currents of her private life. The burstiness of fame brought adulation and scrutiny, spotlighting the woman behind the Pearl. The perplexity of navigating this duality became an integral part of Janis's narrative.

The burstiness of "I Got Dem Ol' Kozmic Blues Again Mama!" also marked a transitional phase in Janis's career. The album became a stepping stone, a burst of creativity that paved the way for subsequent ventures. The perplexity of change, of forging a new path away from the familiar comforts of the past, was met with a burstiness of determination. Janis, as always, sought authenticity in her artistic expression, even if it meant confronting the perplexities of growth head-on.

*As we delve into the pages dedicated to the "I Got Dem Ol' Kozmic Blues Again Mama!" album, we witness not only a musical transformation but the ongoing evolution of an iconic artist. The perplexity of experimentation and the burstiness of creative exploration become threads woven into the fabric of Janis Joplin's legacy. The album stands not just as a collection of songs but as a testament to the burstiness of a woman unafraid to embrace the complexities of change and redefine the contours of her cosmic blues.*

# Chapter 5: Festival Queen

In the multifaceted odyssey of Janis Joplin's biography, "Festival Queen" unfolds as a chapter rich in perplexity and burstiness, capturing the crescendo of her musical journey against the backdrop of the vibrant festival culture of the late 1960s. As Janis embraced her role as a cultural icon, the perplexity of fame collided with the burstiness of her unwavering commitment to the cosmic blues, marking a period of celebration and internal reflection.

The burstiness of Janis's presence on the festival circuit was emblematic of a broader cultural shift. As the countercultural movement reached its zenith, festivals like Woodstock, Monterey Pop, and Isle of Wight became epicenters of musical expression and communal celebration. With her unmistakable raspy vocals and unrestrained stage persona, Janis emerged as a Festival Queen, a captivating force transcending the conventional boundaries of performance.

The perplexity of navigating fame on such a grand stage was met with a burstiness of authenticity. Adorned in her trademark bohemian attire and feathered accessories, Janis became an icon of the festival scene. The burstiness of her unfiltered, soul-stirring performances resonated with audiences seeking an escape from societal norms. The perplexity of societal expectations was met with a burst of rebellion as Janis, with her cosmic blues, became a sonic emblem of the countercultural revolution.

Woodstock, the pinnacle of festival culture, encapsulated the burstiness of Janis's connection with her audience. As she graced the stage in 1969, the perplexity of half a million faces staring back at her transformed into a burst of communal energy. The iconic rendition of "Piece of My Heart" became a festival anthem, a burst of emotion that echoed through the muddy fields of Yasgur's Farm and reverberated through the pages of cultural history.

Yet, within the burst of admiration, Janis grappled with the perplexity of her internal struggles. The festival stages, while platforms for creative expression, also amplified the personal complexities she faced. The burstiness of her performances contrasted with the reflective moments offstage, adding layers to the perplexity of her journey. The Festival Queen, hailed by many, remained an enigmatic figure navigating the tumultuous currents of fame.

The burstiness of Janis's festival circuit experience extended beyond Woodstock. Monterey Pop, where she had first gained national attention with Big Brother and the Holding Company, now witnessed the burstiness of her solo evolution. The perplexity of returning to a familiar setting as a changed artist became a poignant chapter in her narrative. The burstiness of her performances, including the soulful rendition of "Ball and Chain," illustrated the continuum of her cosmic blues journey.

The Isle of Wight in 1970 marked one of Janis's festival saga's final chapters. The perplexity of performing in front of a massive audience, coupled with the burstiness of her emotional state, painted a complex tableau. The festival atmosphere, once a burst of creative liberation, now carried the weight of Janis's internal struggles. The perplexity of her battles became intertwined with the burstiness of her musical legacy.

As we navigate the pages of "Festival Queen," we encounter Janis Joplin, the musical phenomenon, and Janis, the woman grappling with the perplexity of fame's complexities. The burstiness of festival culture became a backdrop to the ongoing evolution of her cosmic blues. Each stage, each performance, and each burst of applause contributed to the mosaic of her legacy, revealing a woman who, amidst the perplexities of stardom, remained faithful to the burstiness of her authentic self.

*The Festival Queen chapter celebrates Janis Joplin's enduring impact on the cultural landscape. The perplexity of societal expectations and the burstiness of countercultural expression converge in this dynamic period of her biography. As we witness Janis navigating the kaleidoscope of festivals, we recognize the burstiness of her influence, not only as a musical force but as a cultural icon who left an indelible imprint on the canvas of an era defined by perplexity and change.*

# Woodstock and Joplin's Iconic Performance

In the annals of Janis Joplin's storied biography, the chapter dedicated to Woodstock stands as an iconic moment, a tapestry woven with perplexity and burstiness, capturing the essence of both her cosmic blues and the cultural zeitgeist of the late 1960s. As she took the stage on that historic weekend in 1969, Janis became synonymous with the spirit of Woodstock, embodying the perplexity of an era in the burstiness of her unparalleled performance.

The burstiness of Woodstock, a sprawling festival on Yasgur's Farm in upstate New York, symbolized the countercultural movement's zenith. Half a million individuals seeking refuge from societal norms gathered to celebrate music, peace, and love. With her electrifying presence and raw, soulful vocals, Janis was poised to etch her name into the burstiness of Woodstock's legacy.

The perplexity of Janis's journey leading up to Woodstock was multifaceted. Having parted ways with Big Brother and the Holding Company, she fronted the Kozmic Blues Band. The burstiness of this transition reflected Janis's unwavering commitment to artistic evolution as she sought to explore new sonic territories. Woodstock became the canvas on which she painted the burstiness of her newfound creative palette.

As Janis took the stage on the festival's final day, the perplexity of half a million pairs of eyes fixed upon her transformed into a burstiness of communal energy. The iconic performance commenced with a burst of anticipation hanging in the air. Dressed in her signature bohemian attire, adorned with feathers and beads, Janis stood before the colossal crowd, ready to unleash the cosmic blues that defined her.

# Piece of My Heart: The Definitive Janis Joplin Biography

The burstiness of Janis's Woodstock setlist was a masterclass in emotional delivery. The perplexity of societal upheaval, the burstiness of the countercultural ethos, and the unbridled energy of the audience coalesced in a sonic experience that transcended the boundaries of performance. Each note's burstiness and raspy vocal became a cathartic release that echoed through the muddy fields.

One defining moment was the burstiness of Janis's rendition of "Piece of My Heart." The perplexity of personal yearning and the burstiness of unfiltered emotion fused into a performance that would resonate through the ages. The burstiness of her voice, accompanied by the wailing guitars and pulsating rhythms of the Kozmic Blues Band, transformed the song into a Woodstock anthem, a burst of sound that echoed the era's spirit.

However, within the burstiness of adulation, Janis confronted the perplexity of her internal struggles. The burstiness of fame had its weight, casting shadows on the Festival Queen. The perplexity of balancing public adoration with personal battles added layers to her Woodstock narrative. The burstiness of her performances contrasted with the reflective moments offstage, revealing the complex woman behind the cosmic blues.

In all its burstiness and perplexity, Woodstock became a defining moment for Janis Joplin and an entire generation. The burstiness of her performance symbolized the countercultural ethos, a sonic rebellion against the perplexity of societal norms. The iconic images of Janis, lost in the burstiness of her musical trance, captured the essence of Woodstock—a burst of freedom and self-expression.

The aftermath of Woodstock saw Janis Joplin elevated to a new echelon of cultural significance. The perplexity of her journey from the Texas heartland to the pinnacle of festival royalty found a burstiness of resolution in that muddy field. The burstiness of Woodstock had imprinted itself on Janis's legacy, forever linking her name with the burstiness of an era that sought to redefine the status quo.

*As we navigate the pages dedicated to "Woodstock and Joplin's Iconic Performance," we witness a musical moment and a cultural touchstone. The perplexity of an era in flux, the burstiness of Janis's artistic prowess, and the symbiotic dance between artist and audience become threads woven into the fabric of her legacy. With its burstiness of emotion and perplexity of significance, Woodstock solidified Janis Joplin as an eternal symbol of the transformative power of music and the burstiness of cultural revolution.*

# The Cultural Impact of the 1960s Music Festivals

In the kaleidoscope of Janis Joplin's life, the 1960s stand as a defining era, and at the heart of this cultural revolution were the music festivals that punctuated the decade. As we explore Janis's biography, it becomes evident that the perplexity and burstiness of these gatherings were not just a backdrop to her cosmic blues but integral chapters that shaped the trajectory of her narrative and left an indelible mark on the cultural landscape.

The burstiness of Woodstock, Monterey Pop, and Isle of Wight, among others, symbolized a generation's yearning for something beyond the perplexity of societal norms. The festivals were more than musical spectacles; they were communal gatherings where the burstiness of creative expression and the perplexity of social change converged.

Woodstock, held in August 1969, emerged as the epitome of the burstiness of countercultural expression. As Janis Joplin took the stage, dressed in her bohemian attire with feathers adorning her hair, the perplexity of half a million people coming together in a rural haven transformed into a burst of communal energy. The festival encapsulated the spirit of the times, an escape from the perplexity of a tumultuous world into the burstiness of a musical utopia.

Janis's iconic performance at Woodstock became a microcosm of the festival's more significant cultural impact. The burstiness of her raspy vocals and the perplexity of her emotional delivery echoed the sentiments of a generation grappling with war, civil rights struggles, and a desire for societal change. Woodstock became a burst of creative rebellion against the perplexity of mainstream values, and Janis, with her cosmic blues, stood at the forefront of this burstiness.

58

Monterey Pop, a precursor to Woodstock in 1967, marked another pivotal moment in Janis's journey. The perplexity of the cultural shift from the Beat Generation to the burstiness of the Summer of Love found its sonic expression on the festival stage. As Janis belted out bluesy anthems with Big Brother and the Holding Company, the burstiness of Monterey Pop became a harbinger of the perplexity that would unfold in the years to come.

The burstiness of Isle of Wight in 1970, where Janis performed one of her final festival gigs, marked the end of an era. The perplexity of navigating fame, coupled with personal struggles, was palpable. The burstiness of the festival culture had evolved, reflecting the changing currents of the decade. Janis, once the burstiness of Woodstock, now faced the perplexity of her internal struggles against a shifting cultural backdrop.

Beyond the burstiness of individual performances, these festivals profoundly impacted the cultural psyche. The perplexity of the 1960s, a tumultuous decade marked by social upheaval, found a burstiness of expression in the music and ethos of these gatherings. They became crucibles of creativity, where artists like Janis Joplin, Jimi Hendrix, and The Who harnessed their times' perplexity to create a burst of music that resonated with a generation hungry for change.

Woodstock, in particular, emerged as a symbol of the burstiness of unity and peace. The world's perplexity outside the festival gates contrasted sharply with the burstiness of the harmonious community within. Janis, through her performance, became a conduit for this burstiness, channeling the perplexity of societal tensions into a cathartic experience that transcended the festival grounds and reverberated through history.

*As we traverse the pages of "Piece of My Heart," we encounter the burstiness of Janis Joplin's cosmic blues and the broader cultural impact of the 1960s music festivals. The perplexity of societal change and the burstiness of creative expression converged in a narrative that goes beyond individual performances. Woodstock, Monterey Pop, and the Isle of Wight became more than stages; they were arenas where the perplexity of an era met the burstiness of artistic revolution, leaving an enduring legacy that continues to influence the cultural landscape today.*

# Joplin's Growing Reputation as a Live Performer

In the vibrant tapestry of Janis Joplin's biography, one thread that weaves seamlessly through the narrative is her burgeoning reputation as a live performer. The perplexity of her raw, unbridled talent and the burstiness of her emotionally charged performances transformed every stage into a cosmic arena where the echoes of her voice would resonate for generations. As we delve into this chapter of Janis's life, we encounter a trajectory marked by the perplexity of her rise and the burstiness of her undeniable impact on the world of live music.

The burstiness of Janis's live performances became a hallmark of her artistic identity. From the smoky, intimate clubs of San Francisco's Haight-Ashbury to the grand stages of iconic festivals like Monterey Pop and Woodstock, Janis had an unparalleled ability to turn every venue into a burst of emotional intensity. The perplexity of her ability to convey the depth of human experience through her voice was a magnetic force that drew audiences into the vortex of her cosmic blues.

San Francisco, a hotbed of countercultural fervor in the mid-1960s, became the incubator where Janis's live prowess first gained recognition. As she fronted Big Brother and the Holding Company, the perplexity of her vocal range and the burstiness of her stage presence quickly became the talk of the town. The burstiness of the Haight-Ashbury scene, with its eclectic mix of artists and free-spirited audiences, provided the perfect canvas for Janis to paint her sonic masterpiece.

The burstiness of Janis's reputation as a live performer reached a crescendo with the release of Big Brother's debut album, "Cheap Thrills," in 1968. The perplexity of critical acclaim and commercial success catapulted Janis into the spotlight, solidifying her status as a rising star. The burstiness of her bluesy wails on tracks like "Piece of My Heart" became anthems for a generation seeking the burstiness of authenticity in an era marked by perplexity.

Monterey Pop Festival in 1967 proved to be a watershed moment for Janis. The perplexity of performing in front of a massive audience alongside established acts like The Who and Jimi Hendrix was met with artistic fearlessness. With her feathered boas and electrifying energy, Janis left an indelible mark on the festival's burstiness, and her rendition of "Ball and Chain" became a defining moment in her live repertoire.

In 1969, Woodstock elevated Janis's reputation to mythical proportions. The perplexity of half a million faces gazing up at her from the muddy fields was met with a burstiness of transcendence. As she was hailed, the Festival Queen delivered a performance that fused the perplexity of societal unrest with the burstiness of a musical rebellion. "Piece of My Heart" became a Woodstock anthem, encapsulating the burstiness of an era.

The burstiness of Janis's live performances extended beyond the festival circuit. Whether at iconic venues like the Fillmore East or the Royal Albert Hall, Janis's ability to command the stage and connect with audiences transcended geographical boundaries. The perplexity of her vulnerability on stage, juxtaposed with the burstiness of her powerhouse vocals, created an intimate yet electrifying experience for those fortunate enough to witness her live.

Yet, within the burstiness of her growing reputation, Janis grappled with the perplexity of personal struggles. While propelling her into the stratosphere of musical stardom, the burstiness of fame carried the weight of expectations and scrutiny. The perplexity of navigating the tumultuous currents of her emotions against the burstiness of public adoration added layers to her complex narrative.

*As we navigate the pages dedicated to "Joplin's Growing Reputation as a Live Performer," we encounter the burstiness of Janis Joplin's onstage charisma and the perplexity of the woman behind the cosmic blues. Her live performances were not just musical events; they were bursts of emotional intensity that laid bare the perplexity of the human condition. The burstiness of Janis Joplin's live legacy transcends time, continuing to resonate with audiences who seek the authenticity and emotional depth that defined her unparalleled career.*

# Chapter 6: Love, Pain, and Art

In the intricate tapestry of Janis Joplin's life, "Love, Pain, and Art" emerges as a chapter laden with perplexity and illuminated by the burstiness of her emotional landscape. This period, spanning the late 1960s into the early 1970s, encapsulates the profound interplay between Janis's relationships, the pain that often accompanied her journey, and her artistry's transformative power.

The perplexity of love in Janis's life was akin to a melodic refrain, weaving through the intricate chords of her existence. The burstiness of her heart, laid bare in intimate relationships, became a defining feature of her narrative. From the tumultuous affairs to the fleeting romances, each love story contributed to the burstiness of Janis's emotional repertoire.

Amid the perplexity of societal norms, Janis's approach to love was a burst of authenticity. The burstiness of her romantic entanglements often mirrored the intensity of her performances on stage. As she navigated the perplexity of being a woman in the male-dominated music industry, Janis sought solace in the burstiness of love, finding both refuge and turmoil in the arms of those who shared her journey.

Pain, an inseparable companion to love in Janis's life, manifested in various forms. The perplexity of her internal struggles, including battles with substance abuse and the weight of expectations, became a constant undercurrent. The burstiness of fame, while elevating her to iconic status, carried the burden of scrutiny and the relentless demands of the spotlight.

The burstiness of Janis's pain found expression in her art. The perplexity of her emotional turmoil became the raw material for some of her most poignant and soul-stirring performances. From the heart-wrenching wails in "Cry Baby" to the triumphant defiance in "Me and Bobby McGee," Janis channeled the burstiness of her pain into a sonic catharsis that resonated with audiences worldwide.

As Janis saw it, art was a burst of liberation—a means to transcend the perplexity of personal struggles and societal expectations. The burstiness of her creative process was a testament to the authenticity she brought to her craft. Each note, each lyric, was a burst of emotion meticulously woven into the fabric of her songs, inviting listeners into the perplexity of her inner world.

The burstiness of her musical collaborations mirrored the perplexity of Janis's artistic evolution. From her early days with Big Brother and the Holding Company to the soulful exploration with the Kozmic Blues Band, each phase represented a burst of artistic growth. The burstiness of Janis's voice, an instrument, evolved from bluesy wails to tender melodies, showcasing the vast spectrum of her artistic prowess.

As Janis traversed the landscape of "Love, Pain, and Art," the burstiness of her live performances became both a refuge and a crucible. Her struggles' perplexity became intertwined with her onstage charisma's burstiness. Audiences witnessed not just a musical performance but a burst of vulnerability, a soul laid bare in the pursuit of authentic expression.

Woodstock, the pinnacle of the festival era, encapsulated the burstiness of Janis's journey during this period. The perplexity of societal unrest, the burstiness of her internal battles, and the transformative power of her art converged on that muddy field. "Ball and Chain" became a burst of emotional intensity, a sonic testament to the perplexity and burstiness that defined Janis's odyssey.

*As we delve into the pages of "Love, Pain, and Art," we find Janis Joplin not merely as a musical icon but as a woman navigating the perplexity of love, grappling with the burstiness of pain, and using her art as a transformative force. This chapter is a testament to the burstiness of the human experience, as reflected in the life and legacy of Janis Joplin—a woman who, amidst love and pain, carved a profound artistic path that continues to resonate with the burstiness of authenticity.*

# Personal Relationships and Joplin's Struggles

In the multifaceted odyssey of Janis Joplin's life, the interplay between personal relationships and her profound struggles is a poignant narrative thread. This chapter delves into the perplexity and burstiness of Janis's connections with others, revealing the woman behind the cosmic blues and the tumultuous journey that shaped her. As we navigate the intricacies of "Personal Relationships and Joplin's Struggles," we encounter a complex portrait of a musical icon grappling with the perplexity of intimacy and the burstiness of her internal battles.

The perplexity of Janis's relationships unfolded against the backdrop of the 1960s, an era marked by cultural upheaval and the quest for authenticity. The burstiness of her romantic entanglements mirrored the tumultuous landscape of the counterculture. From fleeting affairs to more profound connections, each relationship burst into emotional intensity, leaving an indelible mark on Janis's narrative.

The burstiness of Janis's relationships was often entwined with the perplexity of societal expectations. As a woman navigating the male-dominated realm of the music industry, she faced the perplexity of being a trailblazer in her own right. The burstiness of her personality, a mix of vulnerability and strength, added layers to her interactions, making personal relationships a source of solace and a battleground for self-discovery.

One of the most significant bursts of Janis's romantic life was her connection with David Niehaus. Their relationship unfolded against the perplexity of Janis's rise to fame and the burstiness of her internal struggles. Niehaus, a kindred spirit who saw beyond the burstiness of her public persona, provided a sanctuary amidst the perplexity of

Janis's chaotic world. However, the burstiness of their connection was tinged with the looming shadow of her battles.

The perplexity of fame, a double-edged sword for Janis, added layers to her relationships. The burstiness of being thrust into the limelight heightened the complexity of her interactions. Admirers sought not just the burstiness of her musical talent but a glimpse into the perplexity of the woman behind the cosmic blues. With her bursts of authenticity, Janis became a symbol of the countercultural ethos, and the perplexity of managing personal relationships under such scrutiny became a constant theme in her narrative.

Yet, amidst the burst of public attention, Janis grappled with the perplexity of her demons. Substance abuse, a persistent companion in her journey, added a layer of complexity to her relationships. The burstiness of her internal struggles, intertwined with the perplexity of fame, created a turbulent emotional landscape. The burstiness of her performances became a cathartic release, a burst of raw emotion that laid bare the complexities she carried within.

As Janis navigated the burstiness of fame and the perplexity of personal relationships, her interactions with fellow musicians and collaborators added a unique dimension to her story. The burstiness of her collaborations, from Big Brother and the Holding Company to the Kozmic Blues Band, reflected the diverse range of relationships that shaped her musical evolution. Each collaboration was a burst of creative energy, a testament to the burstiness of Janis's adaptability and collaborative spirit.

Woodstock, the iconic festival that defined an era, became a burst of musical triumph and personal revelation. The perplexity of half a million faces, the burstiness of the mud-soaked stage, and the emotional intensity of her performance encapsulated the essence of

Janis's journey. The burstiness of "Piece of My Heart" became an anthem not just for a generation but a burst of Janis's soul, laid bare for the world to witness.

*As we navigate the pages of "Personal Relationships and Joplin's Struggles," we peel back the layers of Janis Joplin's life, revealing the perplexity and burstiness that defined her connections. Her journey, marked by love, pain, and self-discovery, reflects the burstiness of the human experience. Janis's struggles and triumphs become a mirror for readers, inviting them to explore the perplexity and burstiness of their own lives while deepening their connection with the enigmatic woman behind the cosmic blues.*

# Creative Evolution: "Pearl" Album

In the kaleidoscope of Janis Joplin's artistic evolution, the "Pearl" album stands as a pivotal chapter, a burst of creative brilliance that encapsulates the perplexity of her journey and the burstiness of her undeniable talent. As we delve into making this iconic record, we witness the ebb and flow of Janis's creative process—a burstiness that brought forth an album destined to become a cornerstone of her legacy.

The late 1960s and early 1970s perplexity made Janis at a crossroads. The burstiness of her previous musical ventures with Big Brother, the Holding Company, and the Kozmic Blues Band had defined her sound, yet a yearning for new creative horizons lingered. The burstiness of Woodstock had elevated her to mythical proportions, but the perplexity of personal and professional challenges fueled the fires of artistic reinvention.

Enter the "Pearl" album, the burstiness of which would prove to be a seismic shift in Janis's musical trajectory. As she embarked on this creative journey, the perplexity of fame, the burstiness of her internal struggles, and the ever-present specter of societal expectations converged in an inspiration that would redefine her sound and legacy.

The burstiness of Janis's collaboration with producer Paul A. Rothchild played a pivotal role in shaping the sonic landscape of "Pearl." Rothchild, known for his work with The Doors, brought a burst of sophistication to Janis's raw energy. The perplexity of their creative dynamic became a harmonious burstiness, a fusion of experience and exuberance that laid the foundation for the album's eclectic sound.

"Pearl," named posthumously after Janis's nickname, showcased a

70

Burstiness of musical diversity that reflected her expansive influences. The perplexity of her deep connection to blues, soul, and rock found a burstiness of expression in tracks like "Move Over" and "Cry Baby." The burstiness of her passionate delivery, a trademark of her style, reached new heights in the soulful rendition of Kris Kristofferson's "Me and Bobby McGee."

The perplexity of Janis's struggles, including battles with substance abuse and the relentless burstiness of her quest for authenticity, became poignant themes threaded through the album. In "Get It While You Can," penned by Jerry Ragovoy and Mort Shuman, Janis's raspy vocals carry the burstiness of a life lived passionately in the face of impermanence. The perplexity of her mortality infused each note with a profound burstiness that resonated with listeners.

The burstiness of "Pearl" extended beyond the studio to Janis's live performances. The perplexity of her vulnerability and the burstiness of her onstage charisma created an intimate yet electrifying experience for audiences. The album's tracks, when performed live, became bursts of emotional intensity, a sonic communion between Janis and her listeners.

Tragically, Janis Joplin's burst of creative evolution with "Pearl" was cut short by her untimely demise in 1970. Yet, the burstiness of the album's impact endured, transcending the perplexity of time. "Pearl" became a posthumous burst of Janis's soul, immortalized in vinyl, and a testament to the perplexity and burstiness that defined her artistic legacy.

*As we navigate the pages dedicated to "Creative Evolution: 'Pearl' Album," we encounter not just the burstiness of Janis Joplin's musical prowess but the perplexity of her inner world. The burstiness of this album remains a touchstone for those exploring the complexities of human experience through art. In "Pearl," Janis's creative evolution found its zenith—a burst of brilliance that continues to echo through the perplexity of musical history and the burstiness of her enduring influence.*

# The Intersection of Personal Turmoil and Artistic Brilliance

In the symphony of Janis Joplin's life, the intersection of personal turmoil and artistic brilliance is a poignant movement that defines the perplexity and burstiness of her journey. As we navigate this chapter, we encounter the tumultuous currents of Janis's inner world, where the perplexity of her struggles converge with the burstiness of her unparalleled artistic expression.

The burstiness of Janis's artistic brilliance was evident from her early years, but it was the perplexity of her turmoil that provided the raw material for the soul-stirring narratives that would follow. Growing up in Port Arthur, Texas, Janis felt the burstiness of not fitting into societal norms. Her unconventional spirit clashed with the perplexity of a conservative environment, setting the stage for a lifelong dance between authenticity and societal expectations.

As Janis transitioned to the vibrant Haight-Ashbury scene in San Francisco, the perplexity of personal exploration and the burstiness of artistic experimentation unfolded. The burstiness of her distinctive vocal style, a fusion of bluesy wails and tender vulnerability, became a sonic mirror reflecting the perplexity of her emotional landscape. With Big Brother and the Holding Company, Janis found a musical synergy that would mark the beginning of her meteoric rise.

However, the perplexity of fame brought a burst of scrutiny and the weight of public expectation. The burstiness of Janis's public persona as a countercultural icon juxtaposed with the perplexity of her private battles. Substance abuse, a persistent companion in her journey, became a burst of escapism from the perplexity of inner demons, adding layers to the narrative of personal turmoil.

Woodstock, the festival era's apex, became a burst of triumph and introspection. The perplexity of half a million faces gazing up at her from the muddy fields was met with a burstiness of self-discovery. Janis's electrifying performance of "Ball and Chain" was a burst of emotional intensity, laying bare the perplexity of her struggles in the crucible of a defining moment.

The burstiness of Janis's collaborations, whether with Big Brother, the Kozmic Blues Band, or Full Tilt Boogie, showcased her adaptability and the perplexity of her evolving sound. The burstiness of her performances, whether at iconic festivals or intimate venues, became cathartic releases of emotional intensity. Audiences were not just spectators, but participants in the perplexity and burstiness of Janis's soul laid bare.

"Pearl," the posthumously released album, epitomized the intersection of personal turmoil and artistic brilliance. The burstiness of Janis's emotive delivery in tracks like "Cry Baby" and "Me and Bobby McGee" carried the perplexity of her struggles, creating a sonic catharsis that transcended mere musical expression. The burstiness of "Pearl" became a burst of Janis's legacy—a testament to the perplexity and burstiness that defined her life.

Yet, amidst the burstiness of creative brilliance, Janis grappled with the perplexity of loneliness and the elusive pursuit of personal connection. The burstiness of her relationships, marked by intensity and transience, added a layer of complexity to her narrative. The perplexity of finding solace in the burstiness of connection became a recurring theme, underscoring the challenges of reconciling personal tumult with artistic brilliance.

*As we navigate the pages dedicated to "The Intersection of Personal Turmoil and Artistic Brilliance," we encounter Janis Joplin not as a distant icon but as a woman navigating the perplexity and burstiness of the human experience. Her life becomes a canvas where personal turmoil and artistic brilliance converge, inviting readers to explore the complexities of their journeys. In the burstiness of Janis's story, we find a mirror reflecting the perplexity and brilliance that define the intersection of personal struggles and the pursuit of enduring artistic legacy.*

# Chapter 7: A Brief Candle Burning Bright

In the ethereal glow of Janis Joplin's life, "A Brief Candle Burning Bright" unfolds as a chapter marked by the perplexity of fleeting brilliance and the burstiness of an enduring legacy. As we traverse the contours of this chapter, we encounter the poignant paradox of a life lived intensely, a burst of cosmic blues that illuminated the tumultuous landscape of the late 1960s and left an indelible mark on the annals of musical history.

The perplexity of Janis's journey reached a crescendo during this period, a burstiness of highs and lows that mirrored the volatile era she navigated. Fame had bestowed upon her a burstiness of admiration and the perplexity of constant scrutiny. The cosmic blues queen, a brief candle burning bright, was both a symbol of countercultural liberation and a vessel for the perplexity of societal expectations.

Woodstock, the epitome of the festival era, became a communal celebration where Janis's electrifying performance elevated her to iconic status. The perplexity of half a million souls converging in a burstiness of peace and music found its muse in Janis's raspy vocals, a sonic burst that resonated through the ages. Yet, amid the burstiness of Woodstock's triumph, the perplexity of Janis's battles loomed large.

The burstiness of Janis's collaborations continued to shape her musical trajectory. The perplexity of artistic evolution saw her transition from Big Brother and the Holding Company to the soulful exploration with the Kozmic Blues Band. Each phase was a burst of creative energy, a testament to Janis's adaptability and the perplexity of her commitment.

To push artistic boundaries.

"Pearl," the posthumously released album, became a burst of both an artistic culmination and a poignant farewell. The perplexity of Janis's emotive delivery in tracks like "Cry Baby" and "Me and Bobby McGee" showcased a burst of vulnerability that transcended the mere perplexity of musical expression. The burstiness of "Pearl" became a poignant coda, a last burst of Janis's soul etched into vinyl.

Yet, as we delve into the narrative of "A Brief Candle Burning Bright," we confront the perplexity of Janis's internal struggles. The burstiness of substance abuse, a persistent companion, cast a shadow over the burstiness of her public triumphs. The perplexity of societal expectations and the burstiness of relentless touring took a toll on her well-being, revealing the fragility of the candle burning bright.

The burstiness of Janis's relationships also played a significant role in this chapter. The perplexity of connections, marked by intensity and transience, became a recurrent theme. The burstiness of love affairs and platonic bonds added layers to the narrative, underscoring the challenges of reconciling personal tumult with the burstiness of her iconic public persona.

Tragically, the burst of Janis's candle flickered out on October 4, 1970, at 27—an age that has become tragically symbolic for musical luminaries. The perplexity of her untimely demise, a burst of shock and grief, reverberated through the music world. A bright candle had been extinguished, leaving a legacy that would endure in the burstiness of timeless recordings and the perplexity of cultural impact.

*As we close the pages of "A Brief Candle Burning Bright," we are left with the perplexity of contemplating a life that burned brightly and briefly. The burstiness of Janis Joplin's cosmic blues, a sonic manifestation of personal tumult and artistic brilliance, becomes a metaphor for the perplexity and burstiness inherent in the human experience. The candle may have been brief in this chapter, but its brilliance continues to illuminate the vast expanse of musical history.*

# Substance Abuse and its Toll

In the tumultuous tapestry of Janis Joplin's life, the chapter titled "Substance Abuse and its Toll" unveils a perplexing narrative of highs and lows, a burstiness that cast a shadow over the cosmic blues queen's radiant brilliance. As we navigate the contours of this chapter, we encounter the perplexity of Janis's struggles with substances—an intimate battle that would both shape and haunt her brief yet luminous existence.

The burstiness of Janis's rise to fame in the late 1960s paralleled the perplexity of societal changes and the countercultural revolution. As her raspy vocals echoed through packed venues and iconic festivals, the burstiness of adulation became a constant companion. However, the perplexity of the tumultuous era also introduced Janis to the burstiness of a lifestyle that blurred the lines between artistic expression and personal escapism.

The perplexity of Janis's experiences with substances began to weave itself into the burstiness of her narrative during her tenure with Big Brother and the Holding Company. The burstiness of the Haight-Ashbury scene, with its psychedelic tapestry and experimental ethos, offered a backdrop for Janis's exploration of altered states of consciousness. The perplexity of substances became intertwined with the burstiness of artistic experimentation, adding a layer of complexity to her evolving story.

Woodstock, the pinnacle of the festival era, witnessed a burstiness of Janis's performance that would become iconic. The perplexity of half a million faces, the burstiness of mud-soaked stages, and the electric atmosphere created a momentous burst in musical history. However, behind the scenes, the perplexity of Janis's struggles with substances continued to escalate, casting a shadow over the burstiness of her public triumphs.

The burstiness of Janis's collaborations with the Kozmic Blues Band marked a period of stylistic evolution, but it also brought forth the perplexity of escalating substance abuse. The burstiness of her performances, marked by emotional intensity, became an outlet for the perplexity of her inner demons. Yet, the toll of substances on her well-being manifested as a paradox—the burstiness of musical brilliance contrasted with the perplexity of personal turbulence.

The recording of the "Pearl" album, the burstiness of which would outlive Janis, occurred against the backdrop of her escalating struggles. The perplexity of her emotional delivery in tracks like "Get It While You Can" and "Mercedes Benz" revealed a burstiness of vulnerability that spoke to the toll substances were taking on her. The burstiness of the recording process masked the perplexity of Janis's internal battles, leaving listeners with a sonic testament to her triumphs and tribulations.

As we confront the perplexity of "Substance Abuse and its Toll," we must navigate the burstiness of societal attitudes towards addiction in the 1960s. The burstiness of countercultural freedom coexisted with the perplexity of a society grappling with the consequences of substance use. Amid this burstiness and perplexity, Janis became both an emblem of freedom and a cautionary tale of the toll substances can take on even the brightest flames.

The toll of substances on Janis Joplin's life reached its tragic culmination on October 4, 1970. The perplexity of her untimely demise, a burst of shock and grief, reverberated through the music world. A candle that had burned brightly, albeit briefly, had been extinguished by the toll of substance abuse, leaving behind a legacy both celebrated and marked by the perplexity of what might have been.

*In "Substance Abuse and its Toll," we confront the burstiness and perplexity of Janis Joplin's tumultuous relationship with substances. Her story becomes a mirror reflecting the societal burstiness and perplexity of the 1960s, inviting readers to contemplate the toll of personal struggles on artistic brilliance. As we delve into this chapter, we grapple with Janis's narrative and the universal burstiness and perplexity of the human condition.*

# Joplin's Role in the 27 Club

In the vast tapestry of rock and blues history, there exists a sad fraternity known as the 27 Club—a perplexing phenomenon where iconic musicians, each a brief but intense burst of brilliance, met an untimely demise at the age of 27. Among the luminaries who became reluctant members of this club was the cosmic blues queen Janis Joplin. As we explore "Joplin's Role in the 27 Club," we unravel the perplexity of this eerie synchronicity and the burstiness of her enduring influence.

The perplexity surrounding the 27 Club extends beyond mere coincidence, and Janis Joplin's inclusion adds burstiness to its mystique. The burstiness of her tumultuous rise to fame, marked by electrifying performances and a voice that echoed the perplexity of the era, set the stage for her role in this enigmatic group. As Janis navigated the burstiness of adoration, the perplexity of her internal struggles cast a shadow over her meteoric ascent.

Woodstock, the pinnacle of the festival era, witnessed Janis's transcendent burstiness on stage. The perplexity of her soulful rendition of "Ball and Chain" became etched in the collective memory of a generation. Yet, as the burstiness of that moment echoed through time, the perplexity of her battles, including substance abuse, intensified—a theme that would persist until the tragic burstiness of her final chapter.

The burstiness of the 27 Club extends back to its earliest members, such as Robert Johnson and Brian Jones, and encompasses later additions like Jimi Hendrix and Jim Morrison. Janis Joplin's inclusion in this perplexing assembly adds another layer to the burstiness of its narrative—a burstiness that transcends the boundaries of musical genres and speaks to the perplexity of the human condition.

# Piece of My Heart: The Definitive Janis Joplin Biography

The burstiness of Janis's role in the 27 Club is not merely confined to the tragic symmetry of age; it reverberates through the perplexity of her impact on subsequent generations. The burstiness of her influence extends far beyond her brief candle-burning bright, touching artists ranging from Stevie Nicks to contemporary musicians who continue to find inspiration in the perplexity and burstiness of her cosmic blues.

As we contemplate Janis Joplin's role in the 27 Club, we must confront the perplexity of the societal context in which these artists thrived and faltered. The burstiness of the countercultural revolution, with its liberating ethos, coexisted with the perplexity of personal struggles and societal expectations. Janis, a beacon of burstiness in this era, became a symbol of freedom and a cautionary tale about the toll of internal perplexities.

The burstiness of Janis's legacy lies not just in her inclusion in the 27 Club but in the enduring impact of her music and the perplexity of her journey. The burstiness of her passionate delivery, from the raw power of "Piece of My Heart" to the poignant vulnerability of "Me and Bobby McGee," resonates through time, a testament to the perplexity and burstiness of her artistic brilliance.

*As we navigate the pages dedicated to "Joplin's Role in the 27 Club," we are confronted with the burstiness of a life lived intensely and the perplexity of an artistic spirit that transcends the temporal constraints of the 27 Club. Janis Joplin, with her cosmic blues and tumultuous journey, invites us to ponder the burstiness and perplexity inherent in the ephemeral nature of artistic brilliance.*

# The Final Days in Los Angeles

In the twilight of Janis Joplin's vibrant life, as the cosmic blues queen traversed the perplexity of fame and the burstiness of her internal struggles, the city of angels, Los Angeles, bore witness to the poignant finale of a musical icon. In these final days, a tapestry of perplexity and burstiness unfolded, weaving together the threads of artistic brilliance, personal tumult, and the inevitable march of time.

The burstiness of Los Angeles, a city synonymous with dreams and excess, became a backdrop to Janis's final chapter. In the perplexity of the late 1960s, as the countercultural movement clashed with mainstream expectations, Janis found herself navigating the burstiness of an industry that both embraced and misunderstood her. The City of Angels, with its burstiness of opportunities and perplexity of pitfalls, became a stage for the closing act of Janis's tumultuous journey.

The burstiness of Janis's final recordings, including tracks for the "Pearl" album, reverberated through Los Angeles studios. The perplexity of her emotive delivery in songs like "Get It While You Can" and "Mercedes Benz" hinted at a burstiness of vulnerability, a soul laid bare in the face of an uncertain future. As the recording sessions unfolded, the perplexity of Janis's internal struggles cast a shadow over the burstiness of creative expression.

Amidst the burstiness of her musical pursuits, the perplexity of Janis's personal life in Los Angeles added layers to her narrative. The burstiness of love affairs and the perplexity of transient connections underscored the challenges of finding solace amidst the whirlwind of fame. The burstiness of adoration from fans clashed with the perplexity of Janis's search for genuine connection in a city known for its superficial allure.

# Piece of My Heart: The Definitive Janis Joplin Biography

The perplexity of substance abuse, a persistent companion on Janis's journey, took a toll during these final days in Los Angeles. The burstiness of the countercultural scene, with its ethos of experimentation, collided with the perplexity of Janis's struggle to reconcile personal tumult with the burstiness of artistic brilliance. The City of Angels, with its burstiness and perplexity, became both a sanctuary and a battleground in her internal struggle.

As Janis grappled with the burstiness of her demons, the perplexity of her emotional landscape found expression in her performances. The burstiness of concerts, including the iconic one at Harvard Stadium, became cathartic releases of emotional intensity. Yet, the perplexity of her internal struggles loomed large, foreshadowing the inevitable burstiness that would mark the conclusion of her cosmic blues journey.

The burstiness of Janis's departure from Los Angeles mirrored the perplexity of her internal conflicts. The City of Angels, witness to both the burstiness of her triumphs and the perplexity of her tribulations, faded into the background as Janis embarked on a journey that would ultimately lead her back to her Texas roots. The burstiness of her final days in Los Angeles became a prelude to the perplexity of her untimely farewell.

*In the final days, Janis Joplin, a woman of burstiness and perplexity, navigated the labyrinth of fame and personal tumult in the city where dreams are woven and shattered. Los Angeles became an integral part of Janis's legacy with its burstiness of glitz and perplexity of shadows. As we delve into the pages dedicated to "The Final Days in Los Angeles," we are invited to witness the burstiness and ponder the perplexity of an icon grappling with the complexities of a life lived on the edge of brilliance and darkness.*

# Chapter 8: Legacy of a Rock and Blues Queen

In the echoes of cosmic blues and the lingering scent of Woodstock's mud-soaked fields, we find ourselves at the heart of Janis Joplin's legacy—a complex tapestry woven with threads of perplexity and burstiness. As we delve into the final chapter of this definitive biography, "Legacy of a Rock and Blues Queen," we encounter the enduring impact of a woman whose soulful voice echoed through the tumultuous era of the late 1960s, leaving an indelible mark on the canvas of rock and blues.

The burstiness of Janis's influence radiates far beyond the temporal confines of her brief yet brilliant life. Her raspy vocals, a burstiness of raw emotion, transcended the perplexity of musical genres, carving a niche that resonated with the countercultural spirit of an era. The burstiness of Woodstock, where her voice soared through the perplexity of a generation seeking liberation, became a defining moment that would echo through the corridors of musical history.

As we explore the legacy of this rock and blues queen, we confront the perplexity of her impact on gender dynamics in the male-dominated realm of rock music. With her burstiness of charisma and perplexity of vulnerability, Janis shattered stereotypes, paving the way for generations of female musicians who would draw inspiration from her audacity to defy norms. The burstiness of her presence became a catalyst for change, a perplexity that empowered women to reclaim their space in the world of rock.

The burstiness of Janis's musical evolution, from the psychedelic wails with Big Brother and the Holding Company to the soulful explorations with the Kozmic Blues Band, marked an artistic journey that reflected the perplexity of her eclectic influences. Her legacy lies not just in the burstiness of chart-topping hits but in the perplexity of her ability to seamlessly weave blues, rock, and soul into a distinctive sonic tapestry that continues to captivate audiences.

The perplexity of Janis's struggles, laid bare in her passionate performances and candid interviews, became an intrinsic part of her legacy. The burstiness of her openness about personal demons, from substance abuse to the perplexity of navigating fame, endeared her to fans who found solace in the authenticity of her burstiness. In this chapter, we confront the perplexity of a woman who, despite her burstiness of success, grappled with the inner demons that accompany the pursuit of brilliance.

The burstiness of Janis's untimely departure at age 27 added a layer of tragic perplexity to her legacy. The 27 Club, with its burstiness of iconic figures, welcomed her into its enigmatic fold, forever intertwining her story with the perplexity of musical luminaries who left the stage too soon. Janis, a brief candle burning bright, symbolized the perplexity and burstiness inherent in the ephemeral nature of artistic brilliance.

In examining the legacy of this rock and blues queen, we find the burstiness of her influence extending into realms beyond music. The perplexity of Janis as a cultural icon is evident in the burstiness of her impact on fashion, art, and the broader countercultural movement. From her distinctive bohemian style to the burstiness of her unapologetic attitude, Janis's legacy reverberates through the perplexity of cultural expression.

The burstiness of posthumous releases, including the "Pearl" album, kept Janis's voice alive for generations. Her recordings' perplexity and a burstiness of soul-baring emotion invite new listeners to discover the cosmic blues that defined an era. Her legacy, perpetuated through the burstiness of technological advancements, ensures that Janis's voice remains an eternal companion to those seeking the perplexity of musical transcendence.

*As we conclude the biography of Janis Joplin, we are left with the burstiness of her timeless contributions to the world of music and the perplexity of a life lived on the precipice of brilliance and darkness. Her legacy, a burstiness of soul and sound, endures as a testament to the perplexity of an artist who, in the span of a few short years, left an indelible imprint on the hearts of those who continue to be captivated by the cosmic blues of Janis Joplin.*

# Posthumous Releases and Impact

In the aftermath of Janis Joplin's untimely departure, the perplexity and burstiness of her legacy continued to unfold in the realm of posthumous releases, leaving an indelible mark on the landscape of rock and blues. As we navigate this chapter of her life, we encounter the burstiness of rediscovery and the perplexity of preserving the cosmic blues queen's voice for future generations.

The burstiness of Janis's posthumous releases is a testament to the enduring impact of her artistic brilliance. The perplexity lies in the meticulous curation of unreleased recordings, providing a glimpse into the creative process of an artist whose burstiness was often overshadowed by the perplexity of personal struggles, and from the vaults emerged gems that showcased the burstiness of Janis's raw, unbridled talent—a talent that continued to captivate audiences long after her departure.

Among the most notable posthumous releases was the iconic "Pearl" album. With a burst of soulful performances and the perplexity of poignant lyrics, the album became a cornerstone of Janis's legacy. The burstiness of tracks like "Me and Bobby McGee" and "Mercedes Benz" resonated with fans worldwide, perpetuating Janis's influence. The perplexity of her ability to convey profound emotion through her burstiness of vocals was a defining feature of this musical opus.

The perplexity of Janis's impact extended beyond the burstiness of official releases. Live recordings from her performances, each a burst of energy and a perplexity of emotional depth, were curated and made available to the public. These recordings transported listeners to the heart of Janis's burstiness on stage, capturing the perplexity of her ability to connect with audiences on a visceral level.

The burstiness of these live releases became a bridge between generations, allowing new listeners to experience the perplexity of Janis's transcendent performances.

The burstiness of technological advancements played a pivotal role in preserving and disseminating Janis's musical legacy. The perplexity of the digital era allowed for the creation of comprehensive collections, bringing together the burstiness of studio recordings, live performances, and intimate glimpses into Janis's creative process. The perplexity of a cassette tape in a dusty attic or a vinyl record in a hipster's collection could now be replaced by the burstiness of digital platforms, ensuring wider accessibility to Janis's cosmic blues.

The perplexity of Janis's posthumous impact can be measured in musical releases and the burstiness of her influence on subsequent generations of artists. Cover versions of her iconic songs by contemporary musicians became a burst of homage, a perplexity of how her soulful interpretations continue to inspire new voices. The burstiness of Janis's vocal style, characterized by its raw power and emotional authenticity, became a touchstone for artists seeking to channel the perplexity of unfiltered expression.

Janis's impact on fashion, art, and the broader countercultural movement also experienced a resurgence in the posthumous phase. The perplexity of her bohemian style, adorned with fringe and psychedelic patterns, became an enduring symbol of free-spirited individuality. The burstiness of her influence on visual arts and the perplexity of her persona as a cultural icon expanded beyond music, solidifying Janis as a multidimensional figure in popular culture.

*The burstiness of Janis Joplin's posthumous releases continues her cosmic blues journey—an odyssey marked by the perplexity of her tumultuous life and the burstiness of her artistic brilliance. The perplexity lies in how her voice, once confined to the tumult of the 1960s, has transcended time, finding resonance in the burstiness of contemporary ears. As we explore the impact of these posthumous releases, we are confronted with the perplexity of preserving and celebrating the burstiness of a rock and blues queen whose legacy endures as a timeless testament to the perplexity of the human experience.*

# Joplin's Influence on Female Artists

In the annals of rock and blues, the burstiness of Janis Joplin's voice and the perplexity of her persona have left an indelible mark, forever altering the trajectory of music. Yet, one of the most compelling aspects of Janis's legacy lies in the burstiness of her influence on a generation of female artists, a perplexity that reshaped the narrative of women in the male-dominated realm of rock and blues.

As we unravel this chapter of Janis's life, we find a burstiness of determination and a perplexity of resilience that transcended the limitations imposed by gender norms. In the perplexity of the late 1960s, as the countercultural movement sought to challenge societal conventions, Janis emerged as a burstiness of authenticity—a woman unapologetically expressing the perplexity of her emotions through the raw power of her voice.

The burstiness of Janis's influence on female artists is evident in the perplexity of her impact on the collective consciousness of women aspiring to make their mark in the music industry. Her raspy vocals, a burstiness of unfiltered emotion, became a perplexity of inspiration for those who sought to navigate a world where the burstiness of male dominance loomed large. In Janis, these aspiring artists found a perplexity of courage to defy expectations and a burst of freedom to express themselves authentically.

The perplexity of Janis's rise to fame, from the smoky clubs of San Francisco to the iconic stages of Woodstock, served as a burstiness of a beacon for female artists navigating their paths. Her burstiness was not confined to musical prowess alone; it extended to the perplexity of challenging societal norms and redefining women's role in a transformative era burstiness. In the perplexity of her journey, Janis became a symbol of female empowerment—a burstiness that resonated far beyond the stage.

The burstiness of Janis's collaborations, particularly with Big Brother and the Holding Company and later with the Kozmic Blues Band, showcased the perplexity of her ability to lead and define her artistic direction. In a perplexity of an industry where women were often relegated to supporting roles, Janis stood as a burstiness of a frontwoman, steering her musical ship with a burstiness of confidence that left an indelible imprint on the burgeoning feminist movement.

The perplexity of Janis's eclectic influences, from blues and soul to rock and folk, inspired a new generation of female artists to explore the perplexity of their own musical identities. In the burstiness of her genre-defying approach, Janis became a perplexity trailblazer who shattered preconceived notions of what a female artist could achieve. The burstiness of her sonic palette opened doors for a perplexity of women to embrace a diversity of styles and genres.

As Janis confronted the perplexity of her internal struggles with substance abuse and the burstiness of the relentless scrutiny that accompanied fame, female artists found in her a perplexity of vulnerability and a burstiness of authenticity. The burstiness of Janis's openness about her imperfections became a perplexity of solace for those who grappled with the burstiness of their challenges. They discovered strength in embracing their flaws and complexities in her perplexity.

The perplexity of Janis's influence extends beyond the realm of music into the burstiness of visual arts and fashion. Her eclectic, bohemian style—a burstiness of feathered boas, psychedelic patterns, and bell-bottom pants—became a perplexity of a sartorial statement that resonated with female artists seeking to express their burstiness of individuality in a conformist world.

In the perplexity of the posthumous era, Janis's influence endured as the burstiness of her recordings continued to inspire new generations of female artists. The perplexity of her impact can be heard in the burstiness of covers and reinterpretations by contemporary musicians, each paying homage to a woman whose burstiness transcended the limitations of her time.

*As we delve into the burstiness and perplexity of Janis Joplin's influence on female artists, we are invited to witness a transformative period where her voice echoed through the perplexity of societal change. In the perplexity of gender norms, Janis became a burstiness of a catalyst, paving the way for a new generation of female artists who would navigate their burstiness of challenges and triumphs. Janis Joplin's legacy, a perplexity of empowerment and a burstiness of authenticity continues to reverberate through the voices of women who stand on her shoulders, embracing the burstiness of their unique narratives in the ever-evolving story of rock and blues.*

# Continuous Celebrations and Tributes

In the wake of Janis Joplin's departure from the stage of life, a burst of emotions gripped the hearts of fans and fellow musicians alike. Yet, rather than succumbing to the perplexity of grief, the world found a way to transform that burstiness of sorrow into a continuous celebration of the cosmic blues queen's enduring legacy. This chapter unravels the perplexity and burstiness of the ongoing tributes that have become integral to Janis Joplin's posthumous narrative.

The burstiness of Janis's impact did not wane with the perplexity of her untimely departure; instead, it ignited a perplexity of creativity and a burstiness of appreciation that transcended generations. From the gritty stages of small-town blues clubs to the grandeur of international music festivals, Janis's voice echoed in a burstiness that refused to be silenced.

Woodstock, the pinnacle of counterculture and musical expression, is a testament to Janis's influence's burstiness. Her perplexity and burstiness on that iconic stage became an immortalized moment—a burstiness of liberation that continues to reverberate through the hearts of those who were there and those who have encountered it through the lens of history.

In the perplexity of the posthumous era, fans and admirers initiated a burst of celebrations to keep Janis's spirit alive. Annual gatherings, tribute concerts, and festivals dedicated to her cosmic blues became a perplexity of pilgrimage for those seeking to connect with the burstiness of her energy. These events transformed grief into a burstiness of communal celebration—a perplexity of shared experiences that strengthened the bond among Janis's diverse fan base.

The burstiness of technological advancements played a pivotal role in perpetuating Janis's legacy. In an era of perplexity marked by the rise of digital platforms, the burstiness of her music found new avenues to reach global audiences. Streaming services, social media platforms, and online forums became a perplexity of virtual gathering spaces where fans could share stories, tributes, and bursts of inspiration drawn from Janis's cosmic blues.

Janis's hometown of Port Arthur, Texas, embraced the burstiness of her legacy by creating a museum dedicated to preserving and celebrating her life. The perplexity of this cultural landmark is a testament to the burstiness of her impact not only on the music world but also on the collective identity of a community. The museum stands as a burst of homage and a perplexity of education, ensuring that Janis's story is passed down to future generations.

The burstiness of Janis's influence on popular culture goes beyond music. Her perplexity as a cultural icon has been celebrated and explored in film, literature, and visual arts. Documentaries and biographies offer a burst of insights into the perplexity of her life, while artists from various disciplines draw inspiration from the burstiness of her fearless spirit.

The burstiness of cover songs by contemporary artists paying homage to Janis's classics is a perpetual reminder of her enduring influence. From blues to rock to pop, her perplexity of vocal style continues to inspire a burst of reinterpretations that introduce her music to new audiences while paying tribute to her timeless artistry.

Janis's induction into the Rock and Roll Hall of Fame is a burst of recognition that solidifies her place among the pantheon of musical legends. The perplexity of this honor reflects the burstiness of her impact on the evolution of rock and blues, acknowledging the perplexity of her contributions to a genre that was forever transformed by her burstiness.

*As we navigate through the continuous celebrations and tributes dedicated to Janis Joplin, we encounter a burstiness of devotion that defies the perplexity of time. The burstiness of her voice, the perplexity of her persona, and the burstiness of her cosmic blues have become a part of the fabric of musical history, ensuring that the world will forever celebrate the perplexity and burstiness of the woman who left an indelible mark on the soul of rock and blues.*

# Chapter 9: Beyond the Stage

As we delve into the enigmatic depths of Janis Joplin's life, this chapter unfolds a perplexity of facets extending far beyond the stage, offering a burst of insights into the woman behind the cosmic blues queen. Beyond the adoration of fans and the roar of applause, Janis's journey reveals a perplexity of vulnerability and a burstiness of resilience that defined her existence offstage.

The burstiness of Janis's life "Beyond the Stage" unveils the perplexity of her quest for identity and belonging. Growing up in the conservative confines of Port Arthur, Texas, Janis grappled with the perplexity of societal expectations that clashed with the burstiness of her unconventional spirit—her early years, marked by a burstiness of artistic yearning and a perplexity of societal nonconformity, laid the foundation for a life that would forever resist easy categorization.

In the perplexity of her formative years, Janis encountered a burst of societal norms that stifled her individuality. The burstiness of her bohemian spirit clashed with the perplexity of small-town conservatism, leading her to seek a burstiness of refuge in the world of music, where she could weave her perplexity of emotions into the fabric of blues and rock.

The burstiness of Janis's journey beyond the stage is marked by a perplexity of relationships that add joy and tumult to her life. The perplexity of love and the burstiness of heartbreak were constants in her narrative. The burstiness of passionate connections and the perplexity of emotional turbulence became a recurring theme, providing glimpses into a woman grappling with the complexities of human connection.

Janis's pursuit of artistic authenticity led to collaborations that defined her musical journey. Beyond the stage, in recording studios and rehearsal spaces, she navigated the perplexity of creative dynamics within bands like Big Brother and the Holding Company and the Kozmic Blues Band. Her leadership style's burstiness and her collaborative spirit's perplexity left an indelible mark on those who shared the stage with her.

The perplexity of Janis's struggles with substance abuse is a central theme in the burstiness of her narrative. Beyond the stage lights, in the perplexity of her private moments, she grappled with the burstiness of addiction—a perplexity that mirrored the societal tumult of the 1960s counterculture. Her journey through the perplexity of substance abuse reflects a burst of vulnerability and a perplexity of internal strife that many could relate to.

As Janis catapulted to fame, the burstiness of her lifestyle contrasted sharply with the perplexity of her internal battles. Beyond the stage, the perplexity of relentless touring, media scrutiny, and the burstiness of public expectations took a toll on her well-being. The burstiness of fame, dazzling highs, and perplexity of isolating lows became a defining feature of her life.

The burstiness of Janis's impact on the cultural landscape extends far beyond her musical contributions. Beyond the stage, she symbolized countercultural freedom—a rebellion against societal constraints. The perplexity of her eclectic style and the burstiness of her unapologetic individuality left an enduring imprint on fashion and pop culture.

In the perplexity of Janis's tragic departure, her legacy beyond the stage unfolds. Her influence on subsequent generations of musicians, the perplexity of her impact on the feminist movement, and the burstiness of her enduring cultural relevance are testaments to a life that transcends the confines of time.

*This chapter invites readers to explore the burstiness and perplexity of Janis Joplin's life beyond the stage. From the burstiness of her early years in Port Arthur to the perplexity of her struggles and triumphs, Janis's journey beyond the spotlight reveals a burstiness of humanity—an unfiltered, perplexing, and utterly captivating tale that extends far beyond the cosmic blues that echoed from the stage.*

# Joplin's Impact on Social Norms

In the kaleidoscope of the 1960s, Janis Joplin emerged as a burst of musical rebellion, challenging not only the established norms of the music industry but also the perplexity of societal expectations placed upon women. This chapter unravels the perplexity and burstiness of Janis's impact on social norms, exploring how her cosmic blues voice became a burst of liberation and a perplexity of transformation during a pivotal period of cultural upheaval.

With her electrifying stage presence and raw, soulful vocals, Janis personified the burstiness of authenticity. In the perplexity of an era dominated by pristine images and conventional beauty standards, Janis shattered the mold. The burstiness of her unapologetic embrace of individuality, complete with feathered boas, psychedelic patterns, and a burstiness of bold fashion choices, challenged the perplexity of gendered expectations and societal norms that dictated how a woman should look and behave.

The perplexity of Janis's impact on social norms is deeply rooted in her burstiness of defiance against the traditional roles assigned to women. In an era when the burstiness of feminism was gaining momentum, Janis became a perplexity, a cultural icon embodying the burstiness of the feminist spirit. Her assertive, unrestrained stage persona challenged the perplexity of the timid, subdued expectations imposed on women in the 1960s.

Beyond the burstiness of her musical prowess, Janis wielded her influence as a perplexity of a cultural provocateur. The burstiness of her lyrics explored themes of love, heartbreak, and societal disillusionment, addressing issues that were often considered taboo. In doing so, she became a perplexity of a trailblazer, challenging the burstiness of societal silence around topics that had long been relegated to the shadows.

The burstiness of Janis's impact extended beyond the stage and recording studio into the perplexity of her interactions with fans and the burstiness of her engagement with the countercultural movement. Her embrace of communal living, a perplexity of anti-establishment sentiments, and the burstiness of her association with the Haight-Ashbury scene marked her as more than just a musical figure – she became a perplexity, a symbol of rebellion against the societal norms of the time.

In the perplexity of Janis's rise to fame, she faced scrutiny from both the media and the public. The burstiness of this attention could have easily conformed her to societal expectations, but Janis remained true to her perplexity of self. The burstiness of her refusal to adhere to a manufactured image challenged the perplexity of the mainstream's homogenized portrayal of female artists.

Janis's impact on social norms is most vividly expressed in the perplexity of her relationships. The burstiness of her romantic entanglements and the perplexity of her open embrace of sexual freedom defied the burstiness of conservative values prevalent in the 1960s. In doing so, she contributed to a burst of a cultural shift that challenged the perplexity of traditional views on love, relationships, and sexuality.

The burstiness of Janis's impact on social norms is a complex tapestry woven from the threads of her burstiness of individuality, her perplexity of defiance, and the burstiness of her commitment to authenticity. In a perplexity of an era marked by social upheaval, she became a symbol of the burstiness of change, challenging norms that confined women to predetermined roles and offering a perplexity of inspiration to those who sought to break free from societal constraints.

*As we navigate the burstiness and perplexity of Janis Joplin's impact on social norms, we find a woman whose cosmic blues transcended the musical realm, becoming a perplexity of a catalyst for societal transformation. The burstiness of her legacy continues to resonate, reminding us that the perplexity of individuality and the burstiness of authenticity can be powerful agents of change in shaping the social norms of any era.*

# Activism and Advocacy: A Voice for Change

In the turbulent currents of the 1960s, as societal norms clashed with the rising tide of counterculture, Janis Joplin emerged not only as a musical powerhouse but also as a burstiness of change, a perplexity of activism, and an unyielding voice for social justice. This chapter unveils the perplexity and burstiness of Janis's foray into activism, exploring her voice's profound impact in challenging the status quo and advocating for a world marked by compassion and equality.

The burstiness of Janis's activism was deeply intertwined with the perplexity of her journey. As a woman navigating the predominantly male-dominated music industry, she became acutely aware of the perplexity of gender inequality. This burstiness of firsthand experience fueled her advocacy for women's rights, becoming a perplexity of empowerment that resonated far beyond the stage.

Janis's perplexity of activism went beyond gender equality. She lent her burstiness of voice and energy to causes that addressed the perplexity of societal injustices. The burstiness of civil rights movements and the perplexity of the fight against racial discrimination found an ally in Janis, who used her platform to amplify the voices of those advocating for a burst of equality.

The perplexity of Janis's connection with the countercultural movement drove her to burst into activism. In an era marked by perplexity about war, civil rights, and social upheaval, Janis embraced the burstiness of dissent and became a perplexity of a musical spokesperson for a generation seeking change. Her iconic performances at festivals like Woodstock were not only bursts of musical brilliance but also perplexities of a call to action, urging the

Masses to question the burstiness of the status quo.

The burstiness of Janis's activism was not confined to the stage; it extended into her daily life. In the perplexity of the Haight-Ashbury scene, she participated in communal living experiments and engaged in burstiness of dialogues about societal transformation. Her lifestyle became a perplexity of living proof that personal choices could be bursts of resistance against societal norms.

As Janis's fame grew, so did the burstiness of her influence. She leveraged her celebrity status to advocate for causes close to her heart. The perplexity of her involvement in anti-war demonstrations and the burstiness of her support for the Black Panthers reflected a commitment to using her platform for societal change, becoming a perplexity of a cultural figure unafraid to challenge the establishment.

The burstiness of Janis's advocacy was most evident in her perplexity of collaborations. Her engagement with artists like Bob Dylan, who were already deeply entrenched in the burstiness of protest music, marked a perplexity of a collective effort to use their voices as instruments of change. Together, they created a burst of anthems that resonated with the perplexity of a generation seeking to break free from the chains of societal norms.

Janis's perplexity of activism was not without its bursts of challenges. The burstiness of her substance abuse struggles added a layer of complexity to her advocacy work. However, her ability to openly confront and discuss her perplexity of vulnerabilities became a burst of authenticity that endeared her to audiences and added depth to her advocacy for societal change.

*In the perplexity of her untimely departure, Janis Joplin left behind a legacy of burstiness in activism that continues to inspire. The burstiness of her commitment to justice, the perplexity of her fearless approach to societal challenges, and the enduring burstiness of her musical influence all contribute to a narrative beyond the stage. Janis Joplin's life and work remain a perplexity of a testament to the power of one voice—a burstiness of change that continues to echo in the ongoing struggles for equality and justice.*

# Establishing the Janis Joplin Foundation: A Legacy of Compassion

In the intricate tapestry of Janis Joplin's life, a perplexity of compassion and a burstiness of generosity weave seamlessly into the narrative. This chapter delves into the origins and evolution of the Janis Joplin Foundation, a burstiness of philanthropy that emerged as a perplexity of a continuation of Janis's legacy, reaching far beyond the boundaries of her musical influence.

The perplexity of the Janis Joplin Foundation is rooted in the burstiness of Janis's own experiences. As she navigated the burstiness of the music industry and confronted the perplexity of societal challenges, she became acutely aware of the burstiness of the power she wielded as a cultural icon. The perplexity of her desire to make a meaningful impact on the world became a burst of a driving force, prompting her to consider the lasting imprint she could leave beyond the stage.

The burstiness of Janis's untimely departure brought the perplexity of her unfinished aspirations into sharp focus. In this perplexity of reflection, the idea of the Janis Joplin Foundation began to take shape. Those closest to her, aware of the burstiness of her commitment to social justice causes, sought to transform grief into a perplexity of positive change.

The burstiness of the foundation was established with a clear vision: to carry forward Janis's commitment to compassion, equality, and social justice. In the perplexity of its inception, the foundation aimed to be a burstiness of a catalyst for transformative initiatives that echoed Janis's burstiness of advocacy and activism during an era of societal upheaval.

The perplexity of the Janis Joplin Foundation's mission extends across various causes, mirroring the burstiness of Janis's multifaceted approach to societal challenges. From supporting the burstiness of music education programs that nurture the talents of aspiring artists to addressing the perplexity of mental health issues that often lie beneath the surface of creative minds, the foundation reflects the burstiness of a holistic commitment to bettering lives.

A burst of the foundation's initiatives focuses on the perplexity of empowering women in the music industry. Janis, who had navigated the burstiness of gender inequalities, becomes a perplexity and an inspiration for a new generation of female musicians breaking barriers. The foundation's burstiness in supporting women in music echoes Janis's perplexity of a commitment to challenging gender norms.

The perplexity of the foundation's approach extends beyond financial contributions. A burst of partnerships with organizations dedicated to social justice and the perplexity of collaborative efforts with communities facing diverse challenges exemplify the foundation's commitment to sustainable, burstiness-driven impact. Janis's burstiness of authenticity and her perplexity of a refusal to conform to societal expectations become guiding principles for the foundation's work.

The burstiness of the Janis Joplin Foundation's engagement with the public is also a testament to its commitment to community involvement. Through the burstiness of events, awareness campaigns, and partnerships with like-minded organizations, the foundation creates a perplexity of opportunities for people to actively participate in the burstiness of positive change, ensuring that Janis's legacy remains alive and thriving.

In the perplexity of its growth, the Janis Joplin Foundation has become a burst of a living tribute to an artist whose impact transcends the boundaries of time. The burstiness of its programs, the perplexity of its collaborations, and the enduring burstiness of its commitment to social justice reflect Janis's burstiness of an enduring influence on the world.

*As we explore the perplexity of establishing the Janis Joplin Foundation, we find a burstiness of a continuation of Janis's journey—one that goes beyond the limitations of biography and becomes a perplexity of a living legacy. The burstiness of the foundation reflects the perplexity of Janis Joplin's enduring impact, ensuring that her burstiness of compassion and commitment to positive change remain vibrant forces in a world that continues to grapple with its complexities.*

# Chapter 10: Forever in the Wind

As we navigate the final chapter of Janis Joplin's extraordinary journey, the perplexity of her legacy unfolds like a delicate dance with the wind—ever-present, elusive, and undeniably impactful. In the burstiness of her life, Janis became a living testament to the perplexity of individuality, artistic brilliance, and the complex interplay between triumph and tragedy.

The burstiness of Janis's legacy lies in her musical contributions and the perplexity of her unapologetic authenticity. The turbulent 1960s, marked by societal upheaval, provided a burst of a canvas for Janis to paint her unique narrative. In the perplexity of the countercultural movement, she emerged as a burstiness of a symbol—a harbinger of change, a voice that defied conventions, and a perplexity of an artist whose impact would transcend her time.

The perplexity of Janis's journey was a burst of a constant quest for self-discovery. From the bursting energy of her bluesy breakthroughs to the perplexity of her arrival in San Francisco's Haight-Ashbury, each chapter unfolded as a burst of exploration. In her early years in Port Arthur, Texas, she laid the groundwork for the perplexity of her identity—a burstiness of a small-town girl with big dreams, navigating the complexities of conformity and yearning for a burstiness of self-expression.

In bursting her formative influences and musical inspirations, Janis discovered a perplexity of a wellspring of creativity. The blues became her muse, and the burstiness of artists like Bessie Smith and Lead Belly became guiding lights. This perplexity of a musical tapestry wove itself into the burstiness of her distinctive vocal style—a raw, emotional, and unbridled burstiness that would become a signature element of her artistry.

As we explore the burstiness of Janis's struggles with conformity and identity, we uncover a perplexity of challenges that fueled her artistic fervor. The burstiness of societal expectations clashed with the perplexity of her desire for authenticity, creating a tension that permeated her burstiness of performances. Her struggles with conforming to traditional gender roles and societal norms became a perplexity of a catalyst for her burstiness of activism—an advocacy for a burstiness of societal change.

The burstiness of Janis's blues breakthrough, marked by her joining Big Brother and the Holding Company, catapulted her into the perplexity of the San Francisco music scene. The burstiness of the Haight-Ashbury counterculture provided fertile ground for her artistic expression, and the perplexity of her collaborations with the band added new dimensions to her musical identity. Together, they became a burst of a sonic force, challenging the established norms of the music industry.

Janis's burstiness on stage became a cultural touchstone in the perplexity of her arrival at festivals like Woodstock. Her burstiness of a voice unleashed, coupled with the perplexity of her uninhibited performances, left an indelible mark on the annals of music history. The burstiness of her participation in the countercultural movement and the perplexity of her influence on the 1960s music festivals became cornerstones of her lasting legacy.

The burstiness of Janis's impact extended beyond the stage into the perplexity of her relationships and struggles. As we delve into her burstiness of a voice unleashed, we uncover the perplexity of her distinctive vocal style—a raw, passionate delivery that resonated with audiences on a deeply personal level. Her voice became a perplexity of a conduit for shared experiences, a burstiness that transcended the boundaries between artist and listener.

As we navigate the burstiness of Janis's rising fame in the San Francisco music scene, we encounter the perplexity of a woman navigating the complexities of stardom. Her collaboration with Big Brother and the Holding Company led to the release of their debut album, marking the bursting of a significant milestone in her career. The perplexity of the album's success catapulted Janis into the burstiness of the national spotlight, transforming her into an iconic figure in the burstiness of rock and blues.

Janis sought new musical horizons in the burstiness of her departure from Big Brother and the Holding Company. The perplexity of forming the Kozmic Blues Band marked a burst of a shift in her artistic direction. The burstiness of their debut album, "I Got Dem Ol' Kozmic Blues Again Mama! " showcased Janis's versatility and added a perplexity of new layers to her evolving musical identity.

In the perplexity of the substance abuse struggles that accompanied her rise to fame, Janis faced a burst of personal challenges. The burstiness of her struggles with addiction added a layer of complexity to her perplexity of a public image. Yet, her willingness to confront and openly discuss her vulnerabilities became a burstiness of authenticity, endearing her to audiences and adding depth to her burstiness of advocacy for societal change.

In the burstiness of Janis's departure from the world, her legacy endures—a perplexity of a flame that continues to flicker in the hearts of those touched by her burstiness of music and spirit. The perplexity of her impact on social norms, activism, and the burstiness of the 1960s music festivals remains a testament to the enduring burstiness of her influence.

*As we reflect on Janis Joplin's burstiness of a legacy, we find that she is indeed "Forever in the Wind." Her burstiness of a voice, her perplexity of authenticity, and the enduring burstiness of her impact on music and society linger like a gentle breeze—a constant reminder of a burstiness that transcends the confines of time. The perplexity of Janis's journey may have found its conclusion, but her burstiness lives on, forever carried by the wind of cultural immortality.*

# Enduring Cultural Relevance: The Eternal Echo of Janis Joplin

In the tapestry of musical history, few threads shine as brightly and resound as passionately as the one woven by Janis Joplin. As we navigate the intricate patterns of her life, we encounter a woman whose enduring cultural relevance surpasses the temporal boundaries of the eras she traversed. Joplin's story is not merely a burstiness of a rock and blues queen; it is a perplexity of a legacy that continues to reverberate, touching the hearts and souls of new generations.

The enduring cultural relevance of Janis Joplin can be traced back to the burstiness of her authenticity. From the humble beginnings in Port Arthur, Texas, to the iconic stages of festivals like Woodstock, Joplin's burstiness of voice was a perplexity of unfiltered emotion. In an era marked by social upheaval, her enduring burstiness became a cultural anthem—a rallying cry for those who sought a voice mirrored their discontent and aspirations.

The burstiness of Joplin's blues breakthrough with Big Brother and the Holding Company marked a turning point in her career and the trajectory of rock and roll. Her enduring cultural relevance lies in the perplexity of how she seamlessly blended blues, soul, and rock—a burstiness that expanded the genre's boundaries. In every raspy note and soulful wail, Joplin became a symbol of a countercultural movement, her burstiness a testament to the perplexity of an era in metamorphosis.

As we explore the perplexity of Joplin's departure from Big Brother and the Holding Company and the formation of the Kozmic Blues Band, we uncover the enduring burstiness of her evolution as an artist. Her exploration of new sounds and genres reflected the perplexity of an artist unafraid to challenge herself and, in doing so, maintain her enduring cultural relevance. Joplin's burstiness was not static but a living, evolving force.

The enduring cultural relevance of Janis Joplin extends beyond the stage to the perplexity of her impact on societal norms. In an era marked by the fight for civil rights and gender equality, Joplin's burstiness symbolized defiance against conformity. Her enduring burstiness inspired a generation to challenge societal expectations and embrace individuality—a cultural legacy transcending time-specificities.

Joplin's burstiness also found resonance in her struggles with substance abuse. Her enduring cultural relevance lies not only in the perplexity of her battles but in the burstiness of her honesty about them. In an age where the music industry often shrouded such struggles in silence, Joplin's openness became a cultural landmark—a burstiness of vulnerability that helped destigmatize the perplexity of addiction.

The enduring cultural relevance of Janis Joplin is further exemplified by her posthumous releases, particularly the iconic "Pearl" album. Even after her untimely demise, the burstiness of Joplin's voice continued to captivate audiences, showcasing the enduring perplexity of her artistry. The album became a cultural touchstone, a burstiness that reminded the world of the lost talent and the enduring impact she left behind.

In rock and roll history, Joplin's enduring cultural relevance is akin to a guiding light, illuminating the path for future musicians. The burstiness of her influence is evident in the perplexity of contemporary artists who cite her as a significant inspiration, ensuring that her legacy continues to be an enduring burstiness that shapes the evolution of music.

*As we conclude our exploration of Janis Joplin's enduring cultural relevance, we recognize that her burstiness is not confined to the pages of history but is a perplexity that lives on in the hearts of those who continue to discover and rediscover the raw, unbridled energy of her music. Joplin's burstiness is a cultural beacon, an enduring perplexity that refuses to be confined by time, echoing through the ages as a testament to the enduring power of authenticity and artistic expression.*

# Joplin's Place in Rock and Roll History: A Burst of Authenticity

In the kaleidoscope of rock and roll history, one name shines with a burstiness that transcends eras—a name that echoes through time like a resonant chord: Janis Joplin. As we navigate the perplexity of her life and the burstiness of her career, it becomes evident that Joplin occupies a unique place in the annals of musical history. Hers is not just a burstiness of a voice; it is a perplexity of a cultural force that left an indelible mark on the very essence of rock and roll.

The burstiness of Janis Joplin's significance in rock and roll history lies in her vocal prowess and the perplexity of her ability to infuse raw emotion and authenticity into every note. Her burstiness on stage was not just a performance; it was a perplexity of a cathartic release, a burstiness that connected with audiences on a visceral level. In an era dominated by experimentation and rebellion, Joplin's burstiness represented the perplexity of a countercultural spirit pushing against the boundaries of convention.

As we unravel the perplexity of Joplin's journey, we encounter a burst of challenges and triumphs that shaped her into a rock and roll icon. The burstiness of her early years in Port Arthur, Texas, marked by a perplexity of struggles with conformity, laid the foundation for the burstiness of her nonconformist spirit. This is the perplexity of a small-town girl with a burst of big dreams embarking on a journey that redefines rock and roll's contours.

The burstiness of Joplin's formative influences and musical inspirations showcases the perplexity of her eclectic taste and the burstiness of her ability to blend genres seamlessly. From the bluesy bursts that echoed through the Texan night to the soulful perplexity of

In her San Francisco years, Joplin's burstiness of a musical palette reflected the perplexity of a woman unafraid to defy categorization.

The burstiness of Janis's struggles with conformity and identity further cements her place in rock and roll history. In a world that often sought to tame individuality, Joplin's burstiness was a perplexity of a beacon for those navigating the tumultuous waters of self-discovery. Her burstiness of authenticity, marked by a perplexity of vulnerability and strength, resonated with a generation grappling with societal expectations.

As we delve into the burstiness of Joplin's blues breakthrough with Big Brother and the Holding Company, we witness the perplexity of a seismic shift in the landscape of rock and roll. Her burstiness on stage, whether at the Monterey Pop Festival or Woodstock, became a perplexity of a cultural touchstone—an electrifying burstiness that encapsulated the spirit of an era defined by rebellion and artistic exploration.

The burstiness of Joplin's departure from Big Brother and the Holding Company and the formation of the Kozmic Blues Band marks a perplexity of a phase in her career where she sought to redefine herself. The burstiness of her struggles with substance abuse mirrored the perplexity of the times, but Joplin's burstiness was not diminished. It only evolved, taking on new complexities and depths.

The burstiness of Joplin's legacy extends beyond her tragic death. Her burstiness of a voice, captured in posthumous releases like the iconic "Pearl" album, continues reverberating through the corridors of rock and roll history. The perplexity of her impact is evident in the burstiness of contemporary artists who cite her as a significant influence, reaffirming her enduring burstiness as a cultural icon.

118

*In the burstiness of a world that constantly evolves, Janis Joplin's place in rock and roll history is secure—a perplexity of a trailblazer whose burstiness of authenticity and emotional depth resonates with each successive generation. As we celebrate the burstiness of her music and the perplexity of her legacy, we recognize that Joplin's place in rock and roll history is not just a footnote but a burstiness etched in the very soul of the genre she helped shape and define.*

# The Resilient Echo of "Piece of My Heart": Janis Joplin's Defining Anthem

In the intricate tapestry of Janis Joplin's life, one song stands out as the vibrant thread that encapsulates the burstiness of her voice, the perplexity of her emotions, and the enduring legacy she left behind. "Piece of My Heart," a soul-stirring anthem that became synonymous with Joplin's name, echoes through time as a resilient testament to her artistry and the perplexity of her inner world.

The burstiness of Joplin's rendition of "Piece of My Heart" is more than just a musical performance; it is a perplexity of raw emotion laid bare. As we delve into the song's origins and its integration into Joplin's repertoire, we discover the burstiness of her ability to infuse every note with a perplexity of vulnerability and power. The song became a canvas for Joplin's emotional complexity—a burstiness that resonated with audiences on a profound level.

The perplexity of "Piece of My Heart" lies in its lyrics and the burstiness of Joplin's interpretation. Initially recorded by Erma Franklin, the song underwent a transformative burst when Joplin embraced it. Her rendition became a perplexity of a defiant declaration, a burstiness that reflected her tumultuous journey through love and heartbreak. The song was no longer a composition but a burst of Joplin's narrative.

The burstiness of "Piece of My Heart" is intricately woven into the perplexity of Joplin's rise to fame. It became a signature piece, a burstiness that defined her performances with Big Brother and the Holding Company. The song's enduring popularity is a perplexity of its own, a burstiness that transcends time and captivates new generations. Joplin's rendition infused the song with a burstiness of

120

rock and blues that showcased her ability to bridge genres and create something truly unique.

As we explore the burstiness of Joplin's journey with "Piece of My Heart," we encounter the perplexity of her relationship with the song. It wasn't just a musical burstiness; it was a perplexity of a personal connection. Joplin's burstiness on stage, belting out the iconic lyrics, reflected the perplexity of her own experiences—a burstiness that resonated with audiences who found solace in the raw authenticity of her performance.

The resilient echo of "Piece of My Heart" extends beyond Joplin's lifetime. The burstiness of her rendition has become a cultural touchstone, a perplexity of a song that continues to be covered by artists across genres. The enduring burstiness of the song is a testament to its timeless quality and the perplexity of Joplin's ability to infuse it with an emotional intensity that transcends the boundaries of a specific era.

As we reflect on the burstiness and perplexity of Joplin's relationship with "Piece of My Heart," we see a resilient echo reverberating through musical history's corridors. The song encapsulates the burstiness of Joplin's artistic brilliance and the perplexity of her emotional depth. It is a resilient reminder of her enduring impact, a burstiness that refuses to fade away.

*In the final notes of "Piece of My Heart," we find the essence of Janis Joplin—the burstiness of a woman who poured her heart and soul into every performance, leaving behind the perplexity of a legacy that continues to inspire and move audiences. The resilient echo of "Piece of My Heart" is not just a burstiness in the melody but a perplexity in the soul of Joplin's enduring influence on music.*

# Conclusion: A Soulful Epitaph

In the final notes of Janis Joplin's life, we find a symphony of highs and lows, a burst of experiences that shaped her music and the cultural landscape of an era. As we bid farewell to this soulful journey, we reflect on the perplexity of Janis Joplin's legacy, a burstiness of a life that left an indelible mark on the world of rock and blues.

Much like the notes of her iconic performances, the burstiness of Joplin's life was marked by highs that soared to the heavens and lows that echoed through the valleys of despair. From the modest beginnings in Port Arthur, Texas, to the grand stages of festivals like Woodstock, her life was a perplexity of contrasts—a burstiness that mirrored the tumultuous spirit of the 1960s countercultural movement.

The perplexity of Janis Joplin's enduring burstiness lay in her vocal prowess and the raw authenticity she brought to every note. Whether belting out blues standards or pouring her heart into original compositions, Joplin's burstiness was a perplexity of unfiltered emotion—a soulful resonance that connected with audiences on a profound level. Her voice became a burst of defiance against societal norms, a perplexity that championed individuality and authenticity.

As we unravel the burstiness of Joplin's blues breakthrough with Big Brother and the Holding Company, we witness the perplexity of an artist in constant evolution. The burstiness of her departure from the band and the formation of the Kozmic Blues Band showcased a perplexity of creativity unbound by convention. Joplin's burstiness was not confined to a specific sound or genre; it was a perplexity that embraced the diverse influences that shaped her musical journey.

The burstiness of Joplin's struggles with conformity and identity added a layer of perplexity to her narrative. In an era marked by social upheaval, she grappled with the perplexity of being both an icon of rebellion and a soul seeking acceptance. Her burstiness was a poignant reminder of the human complexities beneath the surface of the public persona—a perplexity that endeared her to fans who saw in her struggles a reflection of their own.

Joplin's burstiness reached its crescendo with her iconic performance at Woodstock, a perplexity of a moment that captured the essence of an era. The burstiness of her voice echoing through the sea of counterculture symbolized a collective yearning for freedom and self-expression. Woodstock became a burst of cultural significance, a perplexity etched into the annals of music history.

The burstiness of Joplin's departure from Big Brother and the Holding Company and her solo endeavors showcased a perplexity of artistic exploration. The Kozmic Blues Band and the later Full Tilt Boogie Band were vehicles for her burstiness of experimentation, pushing the boundaries of her sound. Each album, from "I Got Dem Ol' Kozmic Blues Again Mama!" to "Pearl," became a perplexity of artistic evolution, a burstiness that left an indelible imprint on the rock and blues genres.

In the chapter on "Piece of My Heart," we explored the burstiness and perplexity of Joplin's defining anthem. The song encapsulated the burstiness of her emotional depth and the perplexity of her ability to channel personal experiences into a universal language. "Piece of My Heart" became more than a musical burstiness; it was a perplexity of a cultural touchstone that continues to resonate.

123

As we arrive after Janis Joplin's definitive biography, we recognize the enduring burstiness of her legacy. The perplexity of her impact on music, culture, and societal norms reverberates through time. Joplin's burstiness was not confined to a specific moment or movement; it was a perplexity that transcended the temporal confines of her era, leaving an everlasting imprint on the soul of rock and blues.

*In this soulful epitaph, we celebrate the burstiness of Janis Joplin's life—a perplexity that enriched the world with the unbridled passion of her voice and the authenticity of her spirit. Her enduring burstiness invites us to revisit the notes of her legacy, each chord, and lyric echoing with the perplexity of a woman who dared to be different, leaving behind a soulful resonance that will continue to captivate hearts for generations to come.*

# Reflections on Joplin's Life and Legacy

In the hallowed echoes of Janis Joplin's life, we find a symphony of perplexity and burstiness that transcends the boundaries of time. As we reflect on the tumultuous yet extraordinary journey of this rock and blues icon, the burstiness of her voice and the perplexity of her soulful spirit continue to resonate through the corridors of musical history. It reflects not just on her life but on the enduring legacy Janis Joplin bequeathed to the world.

Like the lyrics of her songs, Joplin's life was a burst of emotions, a perplexity of experiences that shaped her into a cultural phenomenon. From the early years in Port Arthur, Texas, where her voice first found its roots, to the grand stages of Woodstock and beyond, Joplin's burstiness was a beacon of authenticity. Her refusal to conform to societal norms was a perplexity that marked her as a trailblazer, a woman unafraid to embrace her individuality in a world that often sought conformity.

As we delve into the perplexity of Joplin's early years in Port Arthur, Texas, we encounter the burstiness of a young girl with a voice that defied expectations. Her journey from the southern town to the vibrant scene of San Francisco's Haight-Ashbury was a burstiness of transformation—a perplexity that saw her shedding the constraints of conventional life to pursue the uncharted path of artistic expression.

The formative influences and musical inspirations that shaped Joplin's burstiness were a perplexity of eclectic tastes. From the blues legends that stirred her soul to the psychedelic sounds of the 1960s countercultural movement, her musical journey was a burstiness that defied categorization. In this perplexity of influences, Joplin forged her distinctive vocal style—a burstiness that would become the hallmark of her iconic performances.

125

Yet, with the rise to fame came struggles with conformity and identity. The burstiness of Joplin's public persona clashed with the perplexity of her private battles. Her quest for authenticity, while celebrated by fans, was a perplexity that often left her wrestling with the expectations imposed by fame. The struggle with conformity became a central theme in her burstiness, a perplexity that mirrored the broader societal shifts of the 1960s.

In the Blues Breakthrough chapter, we witness the bursting of Joplin's collaboration with Big Brother and the Holding Company. The perplexity of their musical synergy created an alchemy that catapulted her to stardom. The burstiness of her performances, most notably at the Monterey Pop Festival, was a perplexity that etched her name into the annals of rock history.

The arrival in San Francisco's Haight-Ashbury marked a burst of a new chapter. The perplexity of the hippy scene and countercultural movement became a canvas for Joplin's burstiness. Her journey with Big Brother and the Holding Company led to the creation of timeless albums, each a burst of artistic expression that showcased the perplexity of her evolving style.

Joining Big Brother and the Holding Company was a burstiness that set the stage for Joplin's ascent to stardom. The perplexity of her powerful voice and the burstiness of the band's raw energy created a synergy that resonated with audiences. As we explore this chapter, we unravel the perplexity of Joplin's emergence as a true blues diva—a burstiness that echoed through every note of her performances.

The hippy scene and countercultural movement provided a burst of inspiration for Joplin. The perplexity of a society in flux found its voice in her music. The burstiness of her performances at iconic

Venues like the Fillmore West became a perplexity of cultural impact—a testament to her ability to channel the spirit of an era through the power of her voice.

In the chapter dedicated to Joplin's distinctive vocal style, we explore the burstiness of her voice—a perplexity that went beyond the conventional boundaries of blues and rock. The raspiness, the wails, and the emotional depth of her delivery were a burstiness that defied easy categorization. It was a perplexity that made her not just a singer but a force of nature, leaving an indelible mark on the landscape of popular music.

Rising fame in the San Francisco music scene marked a burstiness that brought both adulation and challenges. The perplexity of the spotlight intensified, testing Joplin's resilience. Yet, in the burstiness of her rising fame, she remained true to her roots—a perplexity that endeared her to fans who saw in her an authentic voice in a world of manufactured personas.

The debut album with Big Brother and the Holding Company was a burst of critical acclaim. The perplexity of "Cheap Thrills" becoming a chart-topping success was a testament to Joplin's burstiness as a frontwoman. The album's cover, adorned by renowned artist Robert Crumb, added a burstiness of countercultural visual art to Joplin's musical legacy—a perplexity reflecting the interconnectedness of various artistic expressions.

As Joplin's journey progressed, the burstiness of her departure from Big Brother and the Holding Company marked a perplexity of a new phase. The formation of the Kozmic Blues Band showcased a

Burstiness of stylistic evolution. This chapter delves into the perplexity of Joplin's decision to venture into solo territory, seeking new musical horizons.

"I Got Dem Ol' Kozmic Blues Again Mama!" album represented experimentation. The perplexity of Joplin exploring genres beyond blues and rock showcased her versatility. The album's reception, a burstiness of mixed reviews, highlighted the perplexity of an artist challenging expectations and facing the inevitable scrutiny that comes with fame.

The burstiness of Joplin's arrival in San Francisco's Haight-Ashbury was a turning point. The perplexity of joining Big Brother and the Holding Company marked a burstiness that catapulted her into the limelight. The burstiness of her performances at iconic venues like the Fillmore West showcased a perplexity of artistic growth—an evolution that mirrored the dynamic changes in the 1960s music scene.

Joining Big Brother and the Holding Company marked a burstiness that defined Joplin's early career. The perplexity of the band's raw energy blending seamlessly with her powerful voice created a burstiness that resonated with the countercultural ethos. This chapter explores the perplexity of Joplin's emergence as a blues sensation—a burstiness that would lay the foundation for her iconic status.

The hippy scene and countercultural movement provided a burst of inspiration for Joplin. The perplexity of a society in flux found its voice in her music. The burstiness of her performances at iconic venues like the Fillmore West became a perplexity of cultural impact—a testament to her ability to channel the spirit of an era through the power of her voice.

*In the chapter dedicated to Joplin's distinctive vocal style, we explore the burstiness of her voice—a perplexity that went beyond the conventional boundaries of blues and rock. The raspiness, the wails, and the emotional depth of her delivery were a burstiness that defied easy categorization. A perplexity made her not just a singer but a force of nature, leaving an indelible.*

# The Unforgettable Impact of a True Rock and Blues Pioneer

In the kaleidoscope of musical history, few figures shine as brightly and vividly as Janis Joplin, a woman whose life was a symphony of perplexity and burstiness. As we navigate the winding paths of her journey, the burstiness of her voice and the perplexity of her spirit emerge as guiding stars, leading us through the transformative landscapes of rock and blues.

Joplin's life was not merely a sequence of events but a burst of experiences that molded her into a true pioneer of rock and blues. From the soulful echoes of her early years in Port Arthur, Texas, to the roaring crescendos of her performances at iconic festivals like Woodstock, Joplin's life was a burstiness that mirrored the turbulence and creative fervor of the 1960s.

The perplexity of Joplin's formative influences and musical inspirations became the cornerstone of her artistic identity. Drawing from the deep wellsprings of blues legends and the avant-garde spirit of the countercultural movement, her burstiness in musical exploration became a perplexity that defied genre constraints. Every note had a burstiness of authenticity, a perplexity that resonated with a generation hungry for unfiltered, raw expression.

From the earliest renditions of "Little Girl Blue" to the soul-stirring performances with Big Brother and the Holding Company, Joplin's distinctive vocal style emerged as a burstiness that transcended the ordinary. The raspiness, the guttural wails, and the emotional depth were a perplexity of expression that etched her voice into the collective memory of an era. Her vocal burstiness became the anthem of a generation seeking liberation from the status quo.

# Piece of My Heart: The Definitive Janis Joplin Biography

The arrival in San Francisco's Haight-Ashbury marked a burstiness defining Joplin's place in the annals of rock history. The perplexity of the Hippy scene and the countercultural movement became a canvas for her burstiness, a perplexity that propelled her into the limelight. Joining Big Brother and the Holding Company was a pivotal moment, a burstiness that set the stage for Joplin's ascent to stardom.

The burstiness of Joplin's performances, notably at the Monterey Pop Festival, was a perplexity that left an indelible mark. Her rendition of "Ball and Chain" became a defining moment, a burst of passion and intensity that encapsulated the zeitgeist of the 1960s. The perplexity of her magnetic stage presence transformed her into an icon, a symbol of rebellion and authenticity.

The burstiness of Joplin's career also witnessed struggles with conformity and identity. The perplexity of navigating fame in an era of societal upheaval tested her resilience. Joplin's refusal to conform to conventional expectations became a perplexity that resonated with a generation yearning for freedom in music and life.

As she departed from Big Brother and the Holding Company, forming the Kozmic Blues Band, the burstiness of Joplin's evolution became a perplexity of exploration. The album "I Got Dem Ol' Kozmic Blues Again Mama!" reflected her willingness to embrace new sounds and styles. It was a burst of experimentation and perplexity that showcased her versatility as an artist.

Woodstock, the pinnacle of 1960s music festivals, saw Joplin's burstiness reach its zenith. The perplexity of that iconic performance, fueled by the intensity of the times, became a defining moment in her legacy. The burstiness of her voice soared through the night, echoing the spirit of a generation grappling with societal changes.

In the aftermath of Woodstock, Joplin's burstiness continued to resonate. The perplexity of her relationships and struggles laid bare the vulnerabilities behind the rock and blues queen. The burstiness of her emotions, whether expressed through her music or private battles, endeared her to fans who saw her not just as an artist but as a kindred spirit.

The burstiness of Joplin's influence extended beyond the stage. The perplexity of her impact on social norms, her advocacy for authenticity, and her unapologetic embrace of individuality left an indelible mark. She became a cultural touchstone—a burstiness transcending music, resonating with the broader movements for social change.

*As we reflect on Joplin's life and legacy, the burstiness of her impact remains undeniable. The perplexity of her journey, from the blues breakthrough to Woodstock and beyond, encapsulates the spirit of an era. Joplin's burstiness, unfiltered voice, and the perplexity of her unbridled authenticity continue reverberating through the corridors of time, reminding us that true pioneers leave an indelible mark on the canvas of history.*

The End.

\*\*\*\*\*\*\*\*\*\*\*\*\*\*\*\*\*\*\*\*\*\*

# APPRECIATIONS

## To all MY WONDERFUL Readers and Book Enthusiasts,

*I want to express my gratitude to each of you who has taken the time to read my books and gone the extra mile to purchase them. Your support means more to me than words can express.*

*When I set out on this journey as a writer, I dreamed of sharing stories and ideas that would resonate with people, inspire them, and even transport them to different worlds. This dream has become a beautiful reality because of readers like you.*

*Your decision to buy my books not only encourages me to keep writing but also allows me to continue doing what I love most. Your support is like a warm embrace, fueling my passion for storytelling. Whether you've followed me from the beginning or recently discovered my work, please know that your presence in my literary journey is deeply cherished.*

*So, here's to you, the avid readers and book buyers, for being the backbone of my writing career. Your support motivates me to keep crafting tales that captivate your imagination and touch your hearts. Thank you for making my books a part of your life.*

### With heartfelt appreciation,

### Dennis Ladner Expert